MENTOR: Strategies
to Inspire Young People

MENTOR: Strategies to Inspire Young People

Support for Mentors, Educators, Parents, Youth Workers, and Coaches

ROBIN COX

Foreword by
MICHAEL GARRINGER

RESOURCE *Publications* · Eugene, Oregon

MENTOR: STRATEGIES TO INSPIRE YOUNG PEOPLE
Support for Mentors, Educators, Parents, Youth Workers, and Coaches

Copyright © 2024 Robin Cox. All rights reserved. Except for brief quotations in critical publications or reviews, no part of this book may be reproduced in any manner without prior written permission from the publisher. Write: Permissions, Wipf and Stock Publishers, 199 W. 8th Ave., Suite 3, Eugene, OR 97401.

Resource Publications
An Imprint of Wipf and Stock Publishers
199 W. 8th Ave., Suite 3
Eugene, OR 97401

www.wipfandstock.com

PAPERBACK ISBN: 979-8-3852-0133-4
HARDCOVER ISBN: 979-8-3852-0134-1
EBOOK ISBN: 979-8-3852-0135-8

Mural: 'Death Of Innocence' (Annette McGavigan mural) © The Bogside Artists. Image Source: CAIN (cain.ulster.ac.uk/bogsideartists/mural5). Used with permission.

Also, by Robin Cox (more information available at www.yess.co.nz)

On the wings of an Eagle—A young person's guide to successful living

The Mentoring Spirit of the Teacher—Inspiration, support and guidance for aspiring and practicing teacher-mentors

Expanding the Spirit of Mentoring—Simple steps and fun activities for a flourishing peer mentor or peer support program

Nurturing the Spirit of Mentoring—50 fun activities for young people and for peer mentor training

Encouraging the Spirit of Mentoring—50 fun activities for the ongoing training of teacher-mentors, volunteer mentors, student leaders, peer mentors and youth workers

The Spirit of Mentoring—A manual for adult volunteers

Letter 2 a Teen—Becoming the Best I can Be

Making a Difference—The Teacher-Mentor, the Kids and the M.A.D Project

7 Key Qualities of Effective Teachers: Encouragement for Christian Educators

Mentoring Minutes: Weekly Messages to Encourage Anyone Working with Youth

The Barnabas Prayer: Becoming an Encourager in Your Community

CHOICES: Encouraging Youth to Achieve Greatness

Death Of Innocence

Dedicated to the memory of Annette McGavigan
(1 June 1957 – 6 September 1971)[1], whose young life was
tragically cut short during the Irish Troubles, and the millions of
innocent children who have died, or whose lives have
been traumatized in global conflicts.

Blessed are the peacemakers ...
—JESUS

---

1. Appendix 1.

Contents

Foreword xi
Preface xiii
A Mentor's Dream xvii

Section One: The role of a mentor
1. A Cherokee Legend and the spirit of mentoring 3
2. The urgent need for a global youth mentoring strategy 7
3. What is a mentor? 16
4. The three broad stages of a mentoring journey 21
5. Cross-cultural, cross-ethnic mentoring, and understanding youth culture 27
6. Strategies and tips for young people to achieve greatness 31
7. Understand the teenage brain 36
8. Ten mentoring life lessons my students taught me 43
9. How my *ideal* teacher models and promotes the spirit of mentoring 47

Section Two: Strategies and tips to inspire and build meaningful relationships with young people
1. Fun ideas for the mentoring journey 53
2. Discussion topics to build meaningful mentoring relationships 65
3. Responsible use of social media 84
4. How to achieve greatness—winning ways to share with young people 91

Section Three: Mentoring in action
1. Listening to that inner voice—a true story 97
2. Becoming resilient—Barry's story 100

CONTENTS

3. Handling peer pressure—Rachel's, Chris's, and Linda's stories 104
4. Becoming a positive role model—Jason's story 107
5. From teenage rebel to achiever—Jess's story 109
6. Overcoming racial prejudice and adversity—Nick's story 112
7. Social media and youth—Brittany's and Sarah's stories 122
8. Swimming the English Channel—eight life lessons from Trent Grimsey's story 127
9. Strategies and tips to guide teenagers how to overcome adversity—Colin's story 131
10. How to support a teenager who wants to drop out of school 134
11. Handling the highs and lows of stress 137
12. Learning to overcome obstacles with a positive attitude—true stories 140
13. Mentoring moments—through the lens of young people 144

Section Four: Preparing young people for the world of work during the mentoring journey

1. Career thoughts before entering the world of work 151
2. Career-related questions to discuss with young people 154
3. Support a young person to build a winning resume 159
4. Support a young person to create a winning cover letter and portfolio 162
5. Share effective job interview skills for the work place with young people 165
6. Top motivators for employers of young people 169
7. The most important twenty-first-century emotional, entrepreneurial, and employability skills 172
8. The power of the spirit of mentoring—concluding thoughts 175

Appendix 1: Annette McGavigan (1 June 1957 – 6 September 1971) 179
Appendix 2: Mentoring Matters 182
Appendix 3: Advancing the spirit of mentoring: the mixed-age tutor group 184
Bibliography 189

Foreword

While most people can fondly recall the influence of a mentor during their formative years, what often gets overlooked is just how challenging being a mentor to a young person can be! The role of "mentor"—in which a blend of friendship, wise advice, advocacy, teaching, and encouragement is offered to a young person who often has no familial ties to the person providing it—is one of the more nuanced and complex relationships a person can have.

But despite the intimidating complexity of this role, millions of caring adults around the world step into this work every year, forming a new connection with a young person who is often quite different from them, but who could benefit from an additional helping hand on their journey. It is an act of bravery, compassion, community, and, ultimately, love. It is one of the most meaningful ways we adults can nurture the next generation, pass along our wisdom and understanding, and build a just world.

This work is not easy, however, and everyone who steps into the mentor role does so with room to grow in terms of the skills they bring to the relationship, their ability to have meaningful conversations, and their understanding of how to provide the right support at the right moment. Those who mentor through a formal program often get robust training on how to fill this unique role. But the vast majority of the world's mentors are not program volunteers—they are teachers, coaches, faith leaders, co-workers, grandparents, aunties and uncles, next door neighbors. And they need guidance on how to best support the young person in front of them.

This is where a resource like this is invaluable. Robin has collected a lifetime of mentoring wisdom in this book and it offers something meaningful to anyone stepping into this role. While not every mentor will use every strategy or idea in this book, I have no doubt that all people will find value and insight here that will help them be the best mentor they can be. From understanding the role, to tips for getting relationships off to a good start, to figuring out what to do or talk about when spending time with a young person, Robin has collected a roadmap to meaningful relationships and youth thriving.

As the father of two teenagers speeding toward young adulthood, I find his tips for reaching today's adolescents, and helping them transition into the world of work and career, to be particularly salient in helping youth navigate these challenging years.

Regardless of who you mentor or where you do it, I hope you find support, wisdom, and answers to your questions in this resource. The fact that you are holding this book in your hands now means you have a mindset of personal growth and learning that is key for all mentors. Best of luck on your mentoring journey and thank you for bringing more love to the generations to come.

Michael Garringer
Senior Director of Research and Quality, MENTOR

Preface

How do I connect with our young people? What can we talk about? What fun things can we do together? My teenage child seems to be out of control and is not listening to me—help! My mentee seems to be having a brain explosion—help! My mentee comes out of a war situation which I cannot imagine, so how best can I walk alongside her? I can see that my grandchild needs support and encouragement—any tips? My mentee's family recently arrived as refugees, so how can I best walk alongside him? What tips can you give me to be a more effective mentor? She is brilliant on the sports field, but her behavior is inconsistent, and I am concerned about her—help! I don't think my mentoring journey is working—help! My mentee is from a different culture and ethnicity—any supportive tips?

All these questions, statements, and many more thoughts are addressed in this book.

As the global community comes to terms with a pandemic—not forgetting wars, refugee crises, and environmental disasters—that has resulted in the loss of millions of lives, our young people are more vulnerable than ever before.

While some young people might display an "instant gratification" or "entitlement" attitude from time to time, most are strongly influenced by technology—and positive or negative peer pressure—and might also suffer from anxiety, which can negatively impact their ability to reach their potential.

Educators and others working with young people are trying to discern how best to handle the positive and negative aspects of Artificial Intelligence (AI), and technological creations linked to AI.

How many schools, youth mentoring programs, and other education institutions prioritize the importance of developmental face-to-face *relationships*? How many parents work at their face-to-face relationships with their children, upskilling themselves to cope with a variety of parenting challenges?

Three key questions for the twenty-first century might include the following:

i. How do we motivate and inspire the millions of young people who are drifting aimlessly to achieve greatness, or reach their unique potential?

ii. How do we move alongside young people trying to find their way through the confusing adolescent years, made more challenging by a global pandemic, environmental challenges, and the effect of wars?

iii. How do we galvanize communities—especially schools—to develop a global youth mentoring crusade, or an education revolution which places the family—and *face-to-face relationships*—at the heart of the holistic learning journey?

These are some of the questions I regularly ask myself. I have no clear answers. Something must happen to create a global movement which sees the skills, knowledge, and life experiences of millions of potential volunteer adult mentors shared with young people of all ages desperate to have at least one non-judgmental adult in their lives to guide and support them. With the right structures, teachers too can play this significant role, highlighted by the Search Institute's recent research: "Strong student-teacher relationships can be catalytic for student motivation and success in school. Yet too few students experience strong relationships with their teachers."[2]

Indeed, as already mentioned, our challenge is to place the family at the heart of the holistic learning journey. This involves:

- building authentic, effective, and meaningful relationships across all age groups;
- building caring and connected communities;
- creating the most effective conditions for learning and the support of teachers, students, and the families of our young people: a collaborative journey.

---

2. Search Institute, *Developmental Relationships*.

PREFACE

Author Jill Duff writes: "The first sphere of influence, family life, barely gets a mention today, even though it is the biggest determining factor in the wellbeing of children and society."[3]

MENTOR: Strategies to Inspire Young People provides over one thousand tips and strategies to encourage *anyone* walking alongside young people to positively connect with them, and guide them to reach their potential in a meaningful, developmental relationship in line with over twenty-five years of research (Appendix 2).

User-friendly information about the adolescent brain is shared. There are many true mentoring stories from my face-to-face mentoring experiences with over one thousand adolescents over many years, as well as listening to the experiences of hundreds of volunteer adult mentors. These stories give practical meaning to the tips and strategies shared in this book, and in my other mentoring books.

Effective mentors share messages of hope with young people. Through their interactions they guide young people to develop positive and supportive networks around themselves; to cultivate the ability to get alongside others; to become positive people of influence, and to appreciate the importance of having a mentor throughout their life journey—that trusted, non-judgmental cheerleader. Social psychologist, author, and educator, Helen Street, highlights how "positive relationships build students' resiliency and mental health and enhance their capacity for learning."[4]

Committed mentors gain more wisdom and discernment from the mentoring experience. They increase their understanding of what motivates people, and experience further character growth, especially in the area of becoming an empathetic champion of a young person. Mentoring expert Marc Freedman wrote:

> ... mentoring constitutes, in the words of one volunteer, "a window of hope," a glimpse not only of our better selves but of a potentially better society, one built not only on individual acts of kindness, but on a broader set of programs, policies, and institutions that themselves reflect a higher civility.[5]

This book raises the awareness and importance of mentoring young people of all ages—though the focus of this book is more towards teenagers and young adults—and to unlock the "spirit of mentoring" most of us

---

3. Duff, *Lighting the Beacons*, 10.
4. Street, *Contextual Wellbeing*, 109.
5. Freedman, *The Kindness*, xi.

possess at different levels. The Bibliography is a useful starting point for gathering more in-depth information on many of the topics covered.

Repetition is deliberate, as there are a variety of styles and mentoring moments, as well as a specific section or sections a reader might wish to consult at different stages of a mentoring journey. Names of young people have been changed to protect their privacy.

Our young people are the future. Mentors are the wise guides on the side who can inspire them to achieve their potential within a safe, nurturing environment during one of the most confusing and challenging periods of their lives.

Reflect on author Ron Hutchcraft's comment:

> If teenagers had plenty of love and adults who cared, it might not be so critical to invest in a relationship with them. But they are victims of a relationship famine. An adult who cares enough to take the risks of relationship-building can bring so much hope, so much worth into a young person's life … [6]

Robin Cox
New Zealand

---

6. Hutchcraft, *The Battle for a Generation.*

A Mentor's Dream

My dream for you [my mentee] is that you wake up each morning, look at yourself in the mirror, love from the heart the person you see, always strive to be your unique self, and take a positive attitude into every day.

My dream for you is that you build your life on strong foundations, so that you can withstand the inevitable storms of life, and remain a positive person.

My dream for you is that you dare to dream big dreams, set realistic, achievable, and measurable goals, fail sometimes, but remain determined to conquer adversity, and to discover, develop, and use your special gifts and talents to bring about a better community, a more caring society, a more compassionate world.

My dream for you is that you often take time out to reflect on your progress, to visualize yourself ten years from now as a happy, proud, yet humble person, content with life, continually placing the interests of others before your own.

My dream for you is that you discover the meaning of true love; that you sensibly risk entering into positive and meaningful relationships with others, and that your life is wonderfully enriched as a consequence.

My dream for you is that you remember that you are a beautiful person both on the inside and the outside; that you have potential greatness within you, and that, as you leave your footprints on the sands of life's journey, many will walk positively after you, and strive to emulate all that you achieve as a positive person of influence.

My dream for you is that you always remember that you are a special person in God's eyes, and that you discover, during your life's journey, His unique purpose for placing you on this planet.

My dream for you is everything that you positively wish for yourself![7]

7. Cox, *The Spirit of Mentoring*, 24.

SECTION ONE
The role of a mentor

This section includes thoughts about a global youth mentoring strategy to cope with multiple global challenges; provides a broad understanding of the meaning of mentoring; highlights key qualities of effective mentors; provides supportive strategies and tips to connect with the young people with whom we interact, and offers helpful ideas for anyone walking alongside a person of a different cultural or ethnic group. Included are important points about the teenage brain to help us understand the behavior of young people, helpful information about the significance of self-esteem and self-image in adolescence, and strategies and tips to inspire teachers in a mentoring role.

Mentors have opportunities to: increase their mentoring skills, which they can use in numerous personal and professional areas of their lives; learn new technological knowledge and skills; indirectly "pay back" their own mentors for help received; increase their professional network; pass on years of experience; demonstrate their ability to recognize and develop talent; gain tremendous satisfaction from contributing to the development of capable individuals; and possibly gain fresh enthusiasm for their own careers and lives.

—Linda Phillips-Jones[1]

---

1. Phillips-Jones, *The Mentor's Guide*, 5.

1. A Cherokee Legend and the spirit of mentoring

How well do you value the experiences of others?

I recall, as an adolescent, sitting with a variety of influential adults in my life and listening to them share their words of wisdom, though their true stories of the highs and lows of their lives had the most impact on me.

Author Neal Lemery[1] captures stories of young people he has worked with. We gain further insights into the meaning of the spirit of mentoring through his experiential life journey.

Neal shared a well-known Cherokee legend.

> An old Cherokee was teaching his grandson about life. "A fight is going on inside me," he said to the boy. "It is a terrible fight, and it is between two wolves. One is evil. He is anger, envy, sorrow, regret, greed, arrogance, self-pity, resentment, inferiority, lies, false pride, superiority, and ego.
>
> The other is good. He is joy, peace, love, hope, serenity, humility, kindness, benevolence, empathy, generosity, truth, compassion, and faith.
>
> The same fight is going on inside you and inside every person, too."
>
> The grandson thought about his words for a minute, then asked his grandfather, "Which wolf will win?"
>
> The old Cherokee simply replied, "The one you feed."

An effective mentor models both the qualities of the good wolf in their relationship with their mentee, and how to live a healthy and balanced lifestyle. If they are unable to do this, their impact on a mentoring relationship is considerably reduced.

1. Lemery, *Mentoring Boys*.

SECTION ONE: THE ROLE OF A MENTOR

My sport mentors shared the sacrifices they made to achieve their ultimate sporting goals. They taught me about perseverance, and that if I want something I need to work hard at it. I'll probably fail along the way, and that's okay. During these times I learn more about myself and my ambitions, as long as I keep an open mind, and focus on my goal, or goals. Educator, internationally renowned author, and learning consultant Jeannette Vos offers a word of encouragement:

> Look at failure as a patient teacher who never gives up on you and continues working to help you learn no matter how many times it takes. Every time you fail to achieve what you set out to do, reflect on what you did and what you can learn from that experience to bring into your next attempt.[2]

My school history teacher kindly mentored me when I was undergoing my teacher training. His teaching methods, as I later discovered, were far ahead of his time. I continued that legacy with great results, not only with regard to academic results, but also with regard to the quality of the relationships I established with most of the students I taught.

In my penultimate year of school, when the new student leaders for the following year were announced, I felt gutted when my name was not read out. I had worked hard in all areas of my school life, and felt that I had done enough to be appointed. I felt physically ill for about three minutes.

I had a choice to make at that moment. I had missed out on an opportunity. Would I throw in the towel and accept that I would not make the leadership team, or would I continue to work hard in the hope that, later in the new school year, another opportunity might come my way?

It was an easy decision, as I had always enjoyed being part of sport teams in particular. When I was appointed captain of cricket, I had the opportunity to display my leadership capabilities. At the end of a highly successful season both personally and for the team, I was appointed a member of the student leadership group, and achieved another of my goals.

Many of the characteristics required of student leaders in those days were those of the good wolf.

Most young people and adults are impacted by technology and social media. Some might struggle to think beyond themselves, reach out to others, show compassion, empathy, humility, and kindness, while the absence of an authentic faith is also evident.

---

2. Vos, *The Learning Revolution 2.0*.

A CHEROKEE LEGEND AND THE SPIRIT OF MENTORING

When I interact with young people, no matter what their situation might be, at some point I'll steer the conversation towards setting a goal that will result in that young person reaching out to others. It might be doing some chores around the house to raise some money to contribute to a project linked to ending global poverty; or it might involve helping out in some way at a school or club function in the community. There is always a focus on doing something for others. My wife and I have sponsored children and others in different countries for many years. I can also share these experiences with young people, and become a mentoring role model and cheerleader as they choose an outreach project.

Increasingly, adolescent brain research supports the idea that the more we help others, the healthier and happier we ourselves become, hence the importance of continuous dialogue with those we mentor. Clinical professor of psychiatry and author Daniel Siegel noted: "When we have supportive relationships, we are not only happier, we are healthier and live longer."[3]

A final word of support for anyone working with young people from Neal Lemery:

> The little I do—some words of encouragement, a trip to the campus, a visit to a bookstore, a steady hand on his shoulder when the path gets a little rocky—is the best investment I can make in the future. And not just his future. His future successes, smart ideas, and focused leadership are also going to improve my life and make my village a better place to live.
>
> I've received, and I've given back. I've come full circle in the helping-one's-neighbor view of the world. I've seen the planting and the harvest season after season. That kind of farm work—the raising up of others to achieve their dreams and reach for the stars—is what we are here for. In the end of all that care and compassion for our fellow human-kind, we might even end up with a better world for everyone.[4]

Share the story of the Cherokee Legend with mentees. It could open up a variety of discussions, always aimed at encouraging young people to achieve greatness.

---

3. Siegel, *Brainstorm*.
4. Lemery, *Mentoring Boys*.

SECTION ONE: THE ROLE OF A MENTOR

Reflection

Mentors must share not only what their values are, but also explain why they are important, and describe how these values affect their lives. This allows the student to know and understand the mentor .... By sharing, the mentor provides the student with the chance to see a situation from a fresh and different perspective, perhaps for the first time. If this sharing is accomplished without imposing values upon the youth, it can have a positive and lasting effect upon the youth and the relationship.

—BE A MENTOR, INC.[5]

---

5. Be a Mentor, Inc.

2. The urgent need for a global youth mentoring strategy

How many of your family members, friends, work colleagues, acquaintances, or people you know have been impacted negatively by the COVID-19 pandemic? Loss of a loved one? Loss of a job? Loss of a business? Special travel plans dashed?

Perhaps only in time will we understand the deeper impact of COVID-19 on our global community. This thought led me to look at recent research and reports on the impact of COVID-19 on young people. I read articles or reports published in New Zealand, the USA, the United Kingdom (UK), a couple of countries in Eastern Europe, and another by the United Nations Children's Emergency Fund (UNICEF).

What struck me the most was the word *loss*, or words that relayed a similar message of young people losing hope in the future, an increase in anxiety levels, missing being with their friends, feeling more pessimistic about the future, many not asking for help, and others lacking motivation to participate in the activities they usually enjoyed.

There were suggestions that the economic impact of COVID-19 on young people is likely to be long-lasting, as they did not gain critically important income and skill experiences. As prospects dwindle, many face social exclusion, or see their emotional, mental, or physical health deteriorate. The key point, therefore, appears to be that the relationship between economic health and mental health is inextricably linked.

Feedback from the UK Youth movement

An interesting report was produced during the pandemic by the UK Youth[1] movement which surveyed young people and others linked to working

1. UK Youth, *The Impact of COVID-19*.

SECTION ONE: THE ROLE OF A MENTOR

with young people in 2020. This report echoed much of what I read about the impact of COVID-19 in countries around the world. The UK youth movement predicts that, in post-pandemic times, the impact on young people will include the following challenges ranked in order of importance from youth responses:

1. Increased mental health or wellbeing concern.
2. Increased loneliness and isolation.
3. Lack of safe space—including not being able to access their youth club or service, and lack of safe spaces at home.
4. Difficult family relationships.
5. Lack of trusted relationships, or someone to turn to.
6. Increased social media, or online pressure.
7. Higher risk for engaging in gangs, substance misuse, carrying weapons, or other harmful practices.
8. Higher risk for sexual exploitation or grooming.

The report highlights some of the inevitable spin-offs as a result of the impact of the pandemic on the economy such as redundancies in the youth sector, closures of youth-related organizations due to lack of funding, reduced funding, and reduced staff hours. Naturally, should some or all of these developments occur, young people, especially those living in urban environments, will feel more lost, lonely, and at high risk.

Other feedback from and about young people and communities

A report from a USA government department Youth.gov stated: "... more than 1 in 4 young people reported an increase in losing sleep because of worry, feeling unhappy or depressed, feeling constantly under strain, or experiencing a loss of confidence in themselves."[2]

A U.S. government Surgeon General's report on the impact of loneliness and isolation stated:

> Our relationships and interactions with family, friends, colleagues, and neighbors are just some of what create social connection. Our connection with others and our community is also informed by our

---

2. Youth.gov.

neighborhoods, digital environments, schools, and workplaces. Social connection—the structure, function, and quality of our relationships with others—is a critical and underappreciated contributor to individual and population health, community safety, resilience, and prosperity. However, far too many Americans lack social connection in one or more ways, compromising these benefits and leading to poor health and other negative outcomes.[3]

The Global Child Forum provided some challenging thoughts:

> An estimated 99% of children worldwide—or more than 2.3 billion children—live in one of the 186 countries that have implemented some form of restrictions due to COVID-19. Although children are not at a high risk of direct harm from the virus, they are disproportionately affected by its hidden impact. ... For many children the impacts of the pandemic will be catastrophic. ... The pandemic knows no borders, and still it poses a global threat. Our shared humanity demands a global response, and throughout the response and recovery to COVID-19, we must work to protect a generation.[4]

The New Zealand government quoted research that showed evidence that young people are more at risk of adverse psychological, social, health, economic, and educational effects after a disaster such as the COVID-19 pandemic.

Executive coach and author Marshall Goldsmith offers an important insight for anyone working with young people:

> ... our behavior is shaped, both positively and negatively, by our environment—and that a keen appreciation of our environment can dramatically lift not only our motivation, ability, and understanding of the change process, but also our confidence that we can actually do it.[5]

Author and mentoring expert Linda Phillip-Jones highlighted three findings from decades of research by Albert Bandura at Stanford University, as he studied the impact on an individual (a mentee) open to being influenced by a respected, experienced person (a mentor) who showed an interest in, and went out of their way to help that individual.

3. Office of the Surgeon General, *Our Epidemic*.
4. Protect a Generation.
5. Goldsmith, *Triggers*, 5-6.

i. We do most of our learning from observing successful and unsuccessful models. In other words, we watch people's actions, see what happens to them, and then emulate (or avoid) similar actions ourselves.

ii. We respond well to positive reinforcement from certain people. That is, we learn faster and more effectively when we receive positive feedback from someone we respect.

iii. We learn best not only from positive reinforcement, but also from having "mastery" experiences. That means we leap ahead in our learning if we master something difficult.[6]

The significance of self-esteem and self-image in adolescence

Developing a positive self-image and high self-esteem is important during adolescence as young people need to accomplish three key psychological tasks:

1. Develop a sense of *personal identity* that consistently establishes who the young person is through each life role as a unique individual, separate and different from every other individual. This includes the concept of *integrated identity*, meaning that a young person can have many different identities, but they sometimes are not coming together to be a coherent whole. For example, if a young person is an honors student in school, yet also takes part in violent gang behavior, they are unlikely to have a fully integrated identity. Or, if a young person is gay, but in the closet, their identity is not integrated. Mentors can help young people turn these different identities into a unified whole.

2. Begin the process of *establishing committed, intimate relationships*. The young person is asking some important questions which include:

   - Who am I?
   - Where do I come from? (What is my family heritage?)
   - How do I look?
   - Will they like me?
   - Am I too pushy?
   - Will they think I am stuck up?
   - What judgments do I place on myself, and how do I feel about being me?

6. Phillips-Jones, *The Mentor's Guide*, 5.

- What decisions can I actually make and implement about my life and my future? Can I really control my environment?
- What, if anything, is the value of being alive as a human?
- What am I doing here?
- Who is important to me?
- What is life all about?
- What is important to me?

3. Begin making decisions that lead towards *training* and entry into a particular *occupation or profession*.

Whether or not an adolescent completes these three tasks successfully may determine much of what they subsequently accomplish or fail to accomplish. The importance of mentors in facilitating this life journey—as the wise guides on the side—cannot be overemphasized.

An effective youth mentoring global movement

One can spend hours reading similar reports to that of UK Youth and reflecting on the feedback from young people. However, we need to be *solutions focused*, rather than allow ourselves to be dragged into a "doom and gloom" cesspit of negativity. We have millions of Baby Boomers who could be encouraged to move alongside young people to motivate and guide them along a pathway of hope. They can shine a light into the confusion, and possible fear and anxiety of our young people.

Young people in strong, united, stable families with the parent/s actively engaged in their lives are likely to strengthen their resilience. As they learn to master current challenges, their personal growth and development will be noticeable. Researchers at the Search Institute have observed this, and offer further thoughts: "Developmental relationships in families are a source of strength and resilience for many young people. However, they tend to decline through adolescence, and they appear to be more challenging to maintain for families dealing with financial stress." [7]

What of the many young people lacking this parental support, or whose situation changed as a result of the impact of the pandemic on the family's finances? What of the many young people whose families have been caught up in war-torn regions, or those who are refugees for any number

---

7. Search Institute, *Developmental Relationships*.

of reasons, or those who have experienced an environmental disaster, like floods or an earthquake? What role can youth mentoring programs play?

Ten strategies of effective youth mentoring programs

Youth mentoring programs might have different aims depending on the reasons for the respective programs being created, and the young people being targeted, especially those living in high-risk environments. These ten strategies or aims, which are supported by pre- and post-pandemic research, are likely to be common in most programs, and provide a useful check-list for mentors:

1. Help mentees to realize their unique potential.
2. Help mentees to become self-sufficient, productive citizens.
3. Improve the conflict resolution and problem-solving skills of mentees.
4. Guide mentees towards more reliable attendance at school, or study, or work.
5. Improve the social and communication skills of mentees—in relationships with family and extended family, with a focus on behavior, positive attitudes, and appearance.
6. Enhance a sense of social responsibility, together with strong social support, in mentees' lives.
7. Encourage mentees to make positive life choices.
8. Develop positive values and beliefs in mentees.
9. Improve the mentees' self-image and development of positive self-esteem.
10. Expose mentees to new experiences such as community involvement, and engagement with different cultures and activities, so they become positive agents of change in communities.

The power of mentoring

Over the years I have had the privilege of being a mentor to many teenagers from a variety of cultures and ethnicities, and witnessed the powerful impact of mentoring relationships. In my book, *Mentoring Minutes: Weekly*

Messages to Encourage Anyone Guiding Youth[8], I share one of many of these mentoring stories as an example of how a wise and experienced guide moved alongside a vulnerable, unmotivated young person who remained keen to be in a relationship of trust and care, and a life was transformed.

Fifteen-year-old Mason reflected on a nine-month mentoring relationship with his mentor, Ruth, in a school-based mentoring program:

> From this mentoring journey I learnt a lot of things such as, what I wanted to do for my future career and how I was going to achieve the goals I set for myself. The mentoring journey has also shown me how I could improve my life so I wasted a lot less time on things that didn't matter, and I decided to use that time to help myself achieve my long-term goals. I don't think I could have achieved this without the help of my mentor and this mentoring program.

Ruth wrote:

> I have enjoyed sharing this journey with Mason. I have seen him grow in confidence and self-belief. He has made positive changes in his daily life, has discovered a career path that interests him, and has become more assertive. I have enjoyed his sense of humor. I wish him well for his future and know that if he continues to believe in himself, he will accomplish more than he ever dreamed of.

Susan Weinberger, pioneer of school-based or site-based mentoring programs, writes:

> Over the past two decades, site-based mentoring has emerged as a most popular approach to improve the self-esteem, attitudes, attendance, and achievement of school-aged children. Its instant success can be attributed to the program's basic principles. It matches caring adults in the community with youths who could benefit from the attention and long-term relationships. The time commitment is often as little as only one hour a week in a safe, monitored, and supervised environment. The site can be a school, community center, church or agency in a town or city. Mentors like the safety factor, and the one hour spent with the youths is very doable. Together, the mentors and youths, often known as the mentees, decide on the activities in which they will engage.
>
> This initiative has now become a critical intervention across this country [USA], and the benefits are not one-directional. Mentors benefit as much from the experience as their protégés.

---

8. Cox, *Mentoring Minutes*, 22.

SECTION ONE: THE ROLE OF A MENTOR

> Site-based mentoring is one of the most powerful initiatives I have ever witnessed in my 61-year career in the field of education, as a teacher, central office administrator, and consultant.[9]

In recent years more and more neuroscience research has highlighted the importance of young people having meaningful relationships with peers and adults. The importance of goal setting, effective management of time, and living a healthy and balanced lifestyle are increasingly stressed. For example,

> Disconnection, an underlying factor in our society, hits young people the hardest. Mentoring is connection. By getting involved with mentoring, you are helping ensure a bright future for your community and your neighborhood. You will be giving, but also receiving something in return—a big smile, laughter, energy, and a fresh way of looking at the world around you.
> —MENTOR[10]

School communities can be encouraged to set up school-based mentoring programs and peer mentoring—mixed-age—programs; start to think outside the box and take on fresh, new, and proven approaches to educating our young people; encourage the development of creativity, innovative and entrepreneurial thinking, and, where possible, support those youth organizations in their communities—perhaps create partnerships, especially with community youth mentoring programs—undertaking critically important work supporting young people.

As an example of schools becoming agents of change under visionary and selfless leaders, retired school principal Peter Barnard, who advocates a Vertical (mixed-age) Tutoring system in a school community (Appendix 3), which includes the development of peer mentors, stated:

> The mixed-age setting builds collaboration with immediacy from the base. The students in a mixed-age setting are the first to learn how to use the group to change the group in ways that support learning, the start of a domino effect.[11]

After all, to adapt a phrase of American philosopher Frederick Douglas, is it not much better for our communities to build stronger children than to repair broken men and women?

9. Weinberger, *16 Steps*.
10. MENTOR.
11. Barnard, *Socially Collaborative Schools*, 26.

Reflection

You believed in me when no one ever did. Much more than just a teacher or coach. Everyone else saw a delinquent. You saw my talent. God bless you, good man. I wish you all the best. You honestly touched my life. Thank you.

—Student to his former teacher shortly before the latter's death

3. What is a mentor?

I love the definition of a mentor shared by mentoring expert Bobb Biehl: "Mentors are those who have gone before us on the mountain of life, but who pause and extend a hand to help us along the way, or who extend a safety line of love and affirmation that may keep us from falling off the mountain."[1]

The word *mentor*, which has Greek origins, means "a wise guide." Traditionally a mentor was an older, more experienced person who was responsible for training a younger person to fill a particular role. In the Middle Ages, the new generation learned art, craft, and commerce in a master–apprentice relationship, for example, learning the art of making shoes from a shoemaker. Today apprentices continue to learn a trade, or specific job skills from those more experienced than themselves.

A mentor of adolescents takes on a more challenging role than that of a master guiding an apprentice. A mentor should be both a friend and a role model to the mentee at a time in the mentee's life when the influence of peers is of the utmost importance, or when a diligent student from a wealthy area wants to learn how to start a small business, or when the mentee feels devoid of friends, or adult support, or is living in a high-risk environment. A transformational mentor empowers their mentee to be accountable for the choices they make.

> Mentors have come in many forms—as wise elders, as part of extended kinship networks, as spiritual leaders, as teachers and coaches, and as everyday citizens who simply want to offer a helping hand. But regardless of who has stepped into that role, all of these caring adults have played an important part in helping the next generations thrive. … the role of a mentor is unique, as it

---

1. Biehl, *Mentoring*.

speaks to a relationship that is grounded not only in love, but also in common purpose, and with an eye to the future.[2]

Marc Freedman describes how psychologist Uri Bronfenbrenner developed a useful definition of mentoring from his research and consultations with others.

> According to Bronfenbrenner, mentoring is a one-to-one relationship between a pair of unrelated individuals, usually of different ages, and is developmental in nature: "A mentor is an older, more experienced person who seeks to further the development of character and competence in a younger person."[3]

The strategic roles of a mentor

Here are a few helpful strategies and tips to support anyone walking alongside young people. The mentor

Motivates—Motivate and inspire mentees to fulfil their unique potential which they can reach as they develop their own self-worth, and acknowledge the control they have over things that happen to them *most* of the time.

Empowers—Remember that most mentees are powerful without any assistance from an adult. Let mentees know they are valuable and valued. When they feel safe, liked and respected, they feel connected with you. Have realistic yet high expectations, and communicate them. When you empower mentees, you influence them, and *all* the people with whom they interact, including the mentee's family, extended family, and their peers.

Navigates—Become a wise guide as mentees discover more about themselves, come to believe in their own abilities, and deal with a variety of adolescent issues. Be prepared to negotiate clear boundaries with them so that they understand the consequences when they cross these boundaries. Coach them how to learn from mistakes, and understand that failure is part of a lifelong learning experience.

Teaches—Become a coach, role model, and cheerleader whenever possible. A wise guide is a role model who encourages their mentee to develop, or refine important life skills, such as setting and achieving personal

---

2. Herrara and Garringer, *Becoming a Better Mentor*.
3. Freedman, *The Kindness*, 31.

best goals, managing their time effectively, resolving conflicts, appreciating the lasting importance of learning, and having a sense of purpose.

(is) *Open-minded*—Become non-judgmental. Accept mentees as they are. Remain objective—able to look at all sides of an argument or situation—as you encourage mentees to interact positively with others, and learn how to adapt or cope with new situations. Certified neuromuscular therapist Mark Wolynn reminds us that everyone has a story. As the mentoring journey develops, the mentee's life story might be revealed. A mentor might feel that more professional assistance is required for their mentee, and can become the bridge to see this potentially life-changing outcome achieved.

> The great teachers understand that where we come from affects where we go, and that what sits unresolved in our past influences our present. They know that our parents are important, regardless of whether they are good at parenting or not. There's no way around it: the family story is our story. Like it or not, it resides within us.[4]

Reflects—Model the important activity of taking time out to reflect. Teach mentees how to review their situation by looking for the positives, affirming opportunities, and learning from mistakes, and other life experiences. Continue to develop the skill of repeating in your own words something a mentee has shared with you, a great sign to your mentee that you are genuinely listening, and trying to understand what they are sharing with you.

Qualities of mentors as friends

Friendship is at the core of your relationship with your mentee, though this depends on the type of relationship you enjoy with your mentee. There is a difference, for example, between the volunteer adult mentor who is part of a youth mentoring program, and the more professional relationship between a teacher and a student. The teacher would adapt some of these qualities in line with their profession.

Fun-loving—Have lots of fun together, as young people tend to have a wonderful sense of humor. Nurture a sense of humor. Model what it means to laugh at yourself. Coach your mentee not to take themselves or life too

---

4. Wolynn, *It Didn't Start*, 6.

WHAT IS A MENTOR?

seriously. Michael Karcher moves this thinking to a deeper, more holistic level:

> Play is the best way to enter the world of a young person—no matter what age—because doing that extends a sign of respect to youths. Mentors empower people, embolden them, encourage them, and respect them by being playful, because youth know that's their zone. ... What is universal, very healthy, and good to encourage across both genders is the desire to create. Creation in many forms is equivalent to playing in the traditional sense.[5]

Respectful*—Respect both your mentees and yourself as unique beings of great self-worth with a positive self-image. Acknowledge the right of your mentees to make choices, and show them that their opinions and ideas are valued and matter.

Integrity—Be authentic, honest, and truthful at all times. Be consistent and show up on time; be upright, reliable and committed to the relationship, someone your mentees can depend on.

Empathetic*—Place yourself in the shoes of your mentees in order to understand them better. Try to understand *how* your mentee is feeling. Model empathy, and coach your mentee *how* to express empathy in their relationships with family, friends, and other members of the community. Your understanding helps you inspire them to greatness, or to reach their unique potential.

Nurturing—Create a supportive relationship in which your mentees feel cared for, affirmed, and encouraged. Key features in establishing this relationship include being an *effective listener* with a non-judgmental attitude; commit to your mentees; believe in them; be accessible to them, and give of yourself unconditionally. School principal Paul Browning explains: "listening at its best is a selfless act. It is about the other person and not you. It is about entering their world and seeing it from their viewpoint."[6]

Developmental—Encourage your mentees to become the people *they* wish to be, a process that takes time and requires patience, perseverance, and the understanding that developing a friendship also takes time. No "saviors" or "quick fixes" are needed.

Sincere*—Be yourself at all times; be genuine. That is, be aware of your innermost thoughts and feelings, accept them and, when appropriate, share them responsibly (self-expression); know yourself (self-awareness);

---

5. Karcher, *Becoming a Better Mentor.*
6. Browning, *Principled,* 38.

and accept yourself (self-acceptance). Model a spirit of selfless service—serving others, and expecting nothing in return.

* These are the key qualities, or the foundation stones of *any* meaningful relationship.

Reflection

My mentor took me out to lunch for my birthday. After we finished eating, she told me all these things she liked about me, and how she was so glad I was a part of her life. I felt kinda embarrassed, but I've never forgotten what she said.[7]

—14-YEAR-OLD UNKNOWN MENTEE

---

7. Phillips-Jones et al., *100 Ideas*.

4. The three broad stages of a mentoring journey

It is *generally* accepted that the mentoring relationship is a same gender relationship, especially with regard to mentoring teenagers. However, there is often a shortage of male mentors, and so females do mentor teenage boys. If there is a mixed gender relationship, always make sure that the meeting is either in a public place, or in an area where other people are present. This supports the safety and security of both parties.

Mentors are encouraged to take the initiative during the early stages of the mentoring journey. Both you and your mentee are likely to experience feelings of insecurity with each other during those early days—this is normal when two strangers meet for the first time.

Don't expect much response from your mentee initially—small talk is important to them (boyfriends or girlfriends, TV, sport, a party coming up, hobbies, interests, music)—so be patient. Small talk can lead to big talk.

Ask as many open-ended, non-threatening questions as possible. Marshall Goldsmith writes about "active" questions which "focus respondents on what they can do to make a positive difference in the world rather than what the world can do to make a positive difference for them"[1]—a great mentoring strategy.

Turn up and stay in touch. Regular communication with your mentee will enhance the possibility of a positive connection. Be punctual when you meet with your mentee.

Most mentor programs acknowledge that mentoring relationships—especially face-to-face relationships—generally comprise three broad stages:

---

1. Goldsmith, *Triggers*, 108.

SECTION ONE: THE ROLE OF A MENTOR

Stage 1: Getting to know each other

The following are some areas for discussion between a mentor and a mentee for these early meetings as mentors get to know their mentees and vice versa, and a foundation of trust and respect for one another is created:

- Negotiate some ground rules that you will both follow, which include agreement on:
    - confidentiality (adhering to program rules on this matter, as applicable);
    - how often you'll meet face-to-face;
    - the best times to make contact and how you will communicate with each other (cellphone—how often? Negotiated times.). Content? Family rules? Accessibility? Texting (and how this will work)—email, notes, or a combination of these?
    - the role of your mentee's family or caregivers;
    - arrange times to meet (initially consider a three-month schedule).
- Sensitively break down any barriers that may be evident in the relationship.
- Make sure you are both comfortable with the program's expectations of a mentoring relationship (where applicable).
- Discover your mentee's interests and life history, and *have plenty of fun*. If possible, take your mentee on a tour of your old school and share some of your experiences—for example, talk about some of your special teachers, or memorable moments. Then do likewise at your mentee's school, or place of study, or place of work. These experiences can lead to further discussion about what your mentee likes and dislikes about school, work, or further training, and how important your mentee thinks schooling or education is in preparing them for their future career. The discussion gives you an early glimpse into your mentee's values and perspectives on a variety of issues in their life. Alternatively, show your mentee the location of your first job, or first part-time work.
- What are your expectations of this mentoring experience?
- What role would you like me to play as your mentor?

- In what ways can I help or support you?
- Who are the people (adults and peers) who support you best?
- What sort of music do you enjoy listening to? Why? Do you have a favorite singer or group?
- What are your interests or hobbies—how do you spend your free time?

Every mentee and mentor will have a back story. Important questions for the mentor to consider during the early stages of the mentoring journey might include the following:

- Where has my mentee come from?
- Who are the important people in my mentee's life?
- Where does my mentee wish to go?
- What does my mentee need now—any particular struggles or challenges?
- What is my mentee good at (possible strengths)?
- Is my mentee more of an extrovert than an introvert?
- What options are open to my mentee with these skills?
- How can I help and encourage my mentee to develop and extend these skills?
- What is my mentee's worldview?
- How much do I want to share with my mentee? Remember that disclosing information about yourself will help your mentee feel more at ease, and build rapport and trust. You might cover:
    - your occupation, perhaps some career highlights;
    - your favorite interests and hobbies;
    - your personal vision (your picture of yourself); perhaps some goals;
    - some mistakes you've made, and the lessons you learned from them.

Reflection

Nurturing is the foundation of successful mentoring, and the first stage of the relationship has to set the tone between you and the young person you are

SECTION ONE: THE ROLE OF A MENTOR

mentoring. This is the time when you should begin to establish yourself as a role model for your mentee. Talk about your values and back them up with consistent actions. Help your mentee think about what is right and what is wrong. If the young person acts in a way you do not approve of, discuss it and point out more appropriate behavior. Listen to your mentee, encourage them to think about the future, and help to set realistic and attainable goals. The objective of this stage is for you and your mentee to make a strong commitment to the future.

—Dortch Thomas W. Jr.[2]

Stage 2: Setting and achieving goals

Setting and achieving goals in the second stage of the mentoring relationship tends to involve the mentor in:

- forming a closer emotional bond with your mentee;
- doing more fun things with your mentee (which are perhaps more often selected by the mentee), and can sometimes lead to discussions about goal-setting. For example, a mentee loves skate-boarding—what motivates them? Why do they keep getting up and trying again when they fail (perseverance, overcome fear of failure)? How do they feel when they achieve the new trick or task (a goal achieved)?
- guiding your mentee to set some specific, measurable, achievable, limited (within an agreed timeframe), and realistic goals that are initially easy to achieve (to build self-confidence);
- setting some s-t-r-e-t-c-h-i-n-g goals, *chosen by your mentee* ... and encouraging your mentee to achieve them, and not to fear failure;
- praising *effort*, rather than focusing on performance;
- celebrating the small victories;
- understanding that there may be high and low points in the relationship, yet willingly working through such times;
- seeking ongoing support and encouragement from program staff, other mentors, and other resources (as applicable);
- affirming the uniqueness of the relationship;

2. Dortch, *The Miracles of Mentoring*.

- remaining committed to the relationship;
- encouraging your mentee to develop relationships with other positive adults as they learn how to create a supportive network around themselves.

A mentee, who experiences a genuine developmental relationship with their mentor, displays:

- a greater sense of responsibility, reliability, and resilience;
- higher self-esteem;
- stronger relationship-building skills, and they get along better with their parents or caregivers, and teachers (authority figures);
- a more positive attitude to life;
- greater achievement at school, or in their workplace;
- improved academic performance (goal setting skills);
- a clearer direction with career choices;
- reduction in substance abuse, truancy, and inappropriate sexual activities.

Reflection

Shift levels of support. Give more support when young people are struggling, and less when they are making progress. Step back as their skills and confidence build.

—SEARCH INSTITUTE[3]

Stage 3: Reaching closure

A mentoring relationship might suddenly end for a variety of reasons: either the mentor or mentee moves home to another area; personal circumstances change, or a long-term illness is diagnosed. A mentoring relationship should never end leaving a young person feeling they are to blame. We know from research that poorly ended matches hurt young people more than if

---

3. Search Institute, *Developmental Relationships*.

they never had a mentor. When mentoring relationships don't end on a positive note it can be catastrophic for the young person. Some mentoring relationships, often linked to a school or community program, might have a time limit. Whatever the reason or reasons, always do your best to have a final meeting with your mentee, attempting to end the partnership in a *positive, healthy, affirming, and respectful way.*

Author Nikos Kazantzakis aptly describes this role: "Mentors are those who use themselves as bridges, over which they invite their mentees to cross; then having facilitated their crossing, joyfully collapse, encouraging them to create bridges of their own."

Some of the points mentioned below could steer the conversation in the final meeting/s:

- acknowledge the positive effects of the goal setting process;
- where possible, help your mentee plan for the future;
- discuss your mentee's social network as a support base for the future; consider other programs to support their interests or needs;
- review and reflect on the high and low points of the relationship;
- discuss options for staying in touch in the future;
- celebrate the mentoring journey.

Reflection

Adolescence is a period for loosening home ties, exploring the world outside the family, trying out new roles and learning to be independent. Traversing this difficult terrain successfully is facilitated by the presence of trusted adults to whom youths can turn for guidance and support. Through interaction with others, particularly supportive adults, youths acquire the skills necessary for successfully negotiating the world at large.

—Cynthia L. Sipe[4]

---

4. Delpit, *The Politics.*

5. Cross-cultural, cross-ethnic mentoring, and understanding youth culture

What about cross-cultural and cross-ethnic mentoring relationships?

Culture, in its broadest sense, is the underlying fabric that holds together a person's world. In other words, it is just about everything that binds a person to a particular group and time. It includes our language, values, beliefs, customs, rituals, oral and written history, art, music, dance, food, and much more.

The primary job of a mentor is to honor the inherent worth that each young person brings into the world and to respect their special cultural background. Linda Jacovy[1] reminds us that exercising this respect means that mentors will:

- honestly examine their own minds for prejudices and stereotypes (given that almost all of us have learned some);
- think about where their biases come from and try to see them as learned misinformation;
- make a personal commitment to be a culturally responsive mentor who sees their mentee, first and foremost, as a unique and valuable person, and who engages their culture and uses it as a relationship tool;
- approach cultural differences, and diverse ethnic groups as an opportunity for learning.

In addition, Bernadette Sanchez encourages mentors to practice "*cultural humility*, an ongoing, lifelong process of self-reflection and learning about how social identity and experiences are shaped by systems of oppression, power, and privilege."[2]

1. Jucovy, *Same Race and Cross-race Matching*.
2. Sanchez, *Becoming a Better Mentor*.

Sanchez comments that the mentee is the expert of their own desires and interests. My experiences of cross-cultural mentoring have confirmed how much young people enjoy sharing their cultural thoughts and experiences with people with whom they connect.

Key cultural and ethnic bi-directional conversation topics between mentors and mentees

Generally, mentees enjoy sharing cultural values with a mentor. Some possible bi-directional conversation topics in relation to their respective cultural and ethnic values could include the following:

- Who makes up the basic family unit? What are the roles of father, mother, older or younger siblings, and of grandparents, aunts, uncles, cousins?
- How does the family view money which has been earned by a family member? For example, is it shared out within the family? Is a percentage given to faith institutions or other community groups?
- What is your culture's attitude to marriage? Are there arranged marriages? Is dating allowed? Are public displays of affection allowed?
- What communication styles specific to your culture must I be aware of? What forms of greeting are used in your culture? What meanings lie behind various gestures?
- What is your culture's attitude toward teachers or authority in general? Is it disrespectful to challenge such authority?
- What is your cultures attitude to women in authority? For example, in some cultures it is wrong to look directly at a woman.
- What key values are you taught in your culture? What perspectives on time are you taught?
- At what age are you regarded as an adult within your culture? (For example, in South East Asia children are considered to be adults at the age of fifteen years.)
- What is the religion or faith common to your culture or ethnicity?
- How does your culture deal with conflicts? For example, are conflicts resolved directly between the parties involved, or through a mediator, or in some other way?

- What is your culture's attitude to giving and receiving gifts? How does it recognize achievement?
- How should I, as a mentor, behave when I enter your home? What is the protocol? What body language—the way I sit, stand, speak—is appropriate?[3]

Understanding youth culture

It is important to understand the context of your mentee's life so you can understand what they are coping with. Elizabeth Santiago and Minni Chen comment: "It is [also] important to know that their voice, culture, and identity are of equal importance to those of anyone else, including their mentors."[4] Spend some time remembering what it was like to be the age of your mentee. Think about the following questions:

- What was a typical day like?
- What was really important to you at that time?
- What were your parents or caregivers like? Did you get along? Were you close?
- Think of your friends. Were friendships always easy, or were they sometimes hard?
- Were there a number of cliques defined by culture or ethnicity? How did you feel?
- In general, did you feel that adults understood you well?

At the same time, it is important to remember that some things change dramatically, with the result that the new generation may live in a context and have experiences that are vastly different from those of the previous generation. Compared with the time when you were growing up, today there may be, for example, significantly more alcohol and drug abuse; challenges linked to vaping; more widespread and dangerous sexually transmitted diseases; more crime and violence, particularly in urban areas; violence in the media and in "games" as a commonplace event; more single-parent families, and greater demands on all families.

---

3. Cox, *The Spirit of Mentoring*, 94–95.
4. Santiago and Chen, *Becoming a Better Mentor*.

SECTION ONE: THE ROLE OF A MENTOR

The socioeconomic background of your mentee could also differ markedly from your own, although you remain *equals*. Perhaps, for example:

- you own a house, while your mentee's family rents one;
- you own a car, while your mentee travels on public transport;
- you have a TV and DVD player, while your mentee has neither;
- you own a computer, while your mentee has no computer, and has to share a room with two siblings, thus lacking the privacy to work on their own;
- you have lived in the same house for five years, while in the same time your mentee has moved four times.

In other words, remember that many things you take for granted are not necessarily owned or experienced by others.

Poverty may cause stress and depression for your mentee. It may also create a different attitude to money. For example, your mentee might spend $100 on label clothes in order to enjoy the moment, not believing there is any chance of a better future. There is no motivation to save money. However, you can sensitively help your mentees to create a new future for themselves, caring for them in a non-judgmental, unconditional way.

It is important to get to know the individual members of your mentee's family wherever possible. By visiting the family at their home—where this is an accepted aspect of a community youth mentoring program, for example—even getting involved in social activities within the community, you will gain the opportunity to share ideas, views and values, as well as gain a deeper understanding of their culture or ethnic group.

Mentoring expert Thomas Dortch Jr. offers a supportive thought: "Mentoring is a life-affirming circle that has the power to heal the wounds and divisions of our society and that expands every time two people touch each other's lives as mentor and mentee."[5]

Reflection

Mentoring is a brain to pick, an ear to listen, and a push in the right direction.
—John Crosby

5. Dortch, *The Miracles of Mentoring*.

6. Strategies and tips for young people to achieve greatness

My recent research highlights how the pandemic and lockdowns have led to increased anxiety among young people which, if not handled positively and carefully, can lead to depression. This is a reality. Different people will react differently to their environment. So much depends on the individual's experience during the recent pandemic—or other challenging global events—having someone they trust to talk to, or to journey with them as they set new goals, possibly create new dreams, and work hard to create a healthy and balanced lifestyle.

As young people undertake the confusing journey through their teenage years to adulthood, and while their brains are still developing, here are strategies and tips to encourage them to achieve greatness, or to reach their unique potential—come to think of it, they should probably be called *Strategies and tips to achieve greatness*, as they can be adapted to the lives of adults. Anyone guiding young people can use this list as a helpful reference resource.

Attitude—you choose your attitude and how you respond to all that life throws at you. Live in hope, and work hard at taking a positive, constructive attitude into everything you do, and into all your meaningful relationships.

Ask—never stop asking questions no matter how trivial you might think they are. When others share their stories with you, you gain knowledge which could significantly impact your life decisions.

Apologize—no one is perfect. When you make a mistake, say the wrong thing, or forget to do something you promised to do—whatever it might be—front up and be genuinely sorry.

Celebrate—celebrate the small and large victories, the times you achieve a relatively simple goal, or achieve a long-term major goal, or you successfully make it through a tough challenge. Never lose your sense of humor. Laugh often. Have fun.

Communicate—work consistently to develop and improve your communication skills. Become a brilliant listener, a motivator, encourager, and inspiration to others. Develop a positive vocabulary, watch your body language, and radiate care, compassion, and unconditional love towards others. Show empathy, be genuine and respectful, and people will value your contributions to their lives. Always listen respectfully to the opinions and ideas of others. Older people have more life experiences and their stories can assist your personal growth. They were adolescents! Through listening, you have the opportunity to discern information you would like to use, and store, or discard.

Conflict—conflict is part of life. Learn how to turn conflict into a positive learning and growth experience. Deal with it without violating another's rights, and don't run away from it. Develop mediation skills. Become a healer where there is tension, pain, misunderstanding, suffering and trauma—abuse in the home, or by peers—or the everyday horrors of modern economic stress. Peacemakers, who are role models, are desperately needed in our communities.

Failure—never fear failure. Move out of your comfort zone if the challenge is not life-threatening. Life lessons are learnt when you give something a go. The key is to learn from the experience.

Finish well—whatever you do, give it your best shot until you finish, even if this is simply completing something only you know about. Whatever you start, even when you decide it's not something you wish to pursue, finish well. Those who finish well are likely to find that more windows of opportunity open.

Forgiveness—be quick to sincerely forgive those who wrong you, even when you might initially struggle to forget. Be encouraged to discuss the matter with the person or people who have wronged you either directly or in the presence of a mediator. Develop the skills to *positively* resolve conflicts.

Goal getting—be a goal getter. Experiment with different methods of reaching your personal best goal or goals until you find the most effective method that works for you. Draw up a clear action plan, and take small steps initially. Research suggests that those who set personal best goals achieve much.

Humility—stay grounded to avoid your achievements going to your head. Be proud of all you achieve, and always remain unpretentious.

Integrity—be an honest and upright person, someone who keeps their word, and on whom others can depend. Be respectful of yourself and others.

Learning—never stop learning and acquiring knowledge. Knowledge feeds the soul and helps you to become an effective agent of change in your local and wider community. Research, read widely, consult others, and explore the works, ideas, and opinions of others.

Mirror Talk—love the person you see in the mirror each day. Remember, you are unique, special and capable, and no one else has your specific gifts and talents. It is a fact. Never forget that. Ignore those who tell you otherwise.

Money—avoid making money your god. While it's wonderful to have sufficient money to feed, clothe, house, and educate ourselves, later to raise a family in a safe and secure environment, money is unlikely to buy you happiness, nor will owning the biggest and best TV, cellphone, or latest technology gadget. How will you spend money? Consider how you can contribute financially, for example, to end global poverty and, as you do so, it's likely you will make a positive contribution towards solving other global and environmental issues.

Opportunities—engrave into your being that every obstacle can be turned into an opportunity if you are prepared to think creatively, seek the guidance and wisdom of others, and have the patience to work towards something, rather than expect a quick-fix solution, or instant gratification.

Passion/s—identify your passion or passions, or your purpose that gives your life deeper meaning. If you could do *anything* you wanted today and had all the qualifications you needed, what would you choose to do? That's your passion. Do something with it. Chase it!

Persevere—don't quit. Go the extra mile even if you have to sweat a little, make some sacrifices (of social life), or commit yourself to something for a little longer. You will amaze yourself at what you can achieve when you do this.

SECTION ONE: THE ROLE OF A MENTOR

Positive peers—when you surround yourself with positive peers you have a greater chance of fulfilling your potential. Positive peers know right from wrong. Choose your friends carefully, and let trust develop over time.

Reflect—take time out each day to think about how you are doing, what you are doing, why you are doing it, and what lessons can be learnt. Pray, meditate, and be still for a few minutes each day.

Relationships—keep building your relationships and networks with peers, family, other adults (teachers, coaches, or mentors), employers and, most important, with God—that's a challenge, but the soul needs to be nurtured, so don't ignore the exploration and development of your faith.

Self-discipline—build a disciplined lifestyle into all you do. For example, sleep for a minimum of nine hours *every* night; live a healthy and balanced lifestyle (at least thirty minutes of exercise every second day) and watch your diet; manage your time well (time to work, time to study, time to eat, time to socialize and relax, time to exercise, time to follow an interest or hobby, time to sleep); say *no* to substance abuse (so you don't damage your brain during crucial developmental times), cigarettes, vaping, and inappropriate antisocial behavior.

Service—give of yourself to others, and expect nothing in return. Become involved in community outreach programs. As you reach out to others unselfishly, you discover more positive qualities about yourself. Sometimes a friendly smile directed at a stranger or a peer can change their day. The world needs servant leaders—become one.

Share—share your ideals, passions, and goals with at least one adult you trust and respect, in addition to your parents or caregivers. This is your non-judgmental cheerleader who can guide and encourage you to achieve your dreams. This experience also teaches you how to be vulnerable with others in a safe and secure environment, a necessary life skill.

Stay focused—keep your eyes on your personal photograph at all times (see visualization below). That will get you through the tough and challenging times. There are no quick-fix, easy solutions. Success requires consistently hard work, careful planning, and perseverance. *Never* be afraid to fail while daring greatly.

Take ownership—write down your goals in the *present* tense—as if you are achieving them today. Take ownership of your feelings: "*I feel ... because ...*"

Teamwork—always seek to be a team player, a sure way to develop positive peer relationships; have positive role models in your life; be a support to others; turn obstacles into opportunities, and reach out to those in need.

Thanks—always express your genuine thanks to all who share their gold nuggets of wisdom and experience with you, or offer you a helping hand.

Validate—acknowledge the worthiness of the other person, for example, if they share something deeply personal; or if they appear confused or unsure of the next step, or even what they might actually want.

Visualize—create an imaginary photo (or a real one) of yourself achieving whatever it is you would like to achieve—as though you have already achieved it. Note your body language, your facial expression, your positive thoughts—never let go of this photo. Refer to it often, especially during those times when you doubt yourself.

Reflection

Practice your relationship-building skills. You will need them. While computers and AI technology can do some jobs, human interaction will always be needed. In fact, to achieve your dreams, you'll require other people to help you. Therefore, your emotional intelligence will become one of the most important skills you can develop, aside from the skills of self-learning and problem-solving. Emotional intelligence involves understanding why people behave the way they do and how to influence that behavior to get you what you want without hurting yourself.

—JEANNETTE VOS[1]

---

1. Vos, *The Learning Revolution 2.0*.

7. Understand the teenage brain

Do you sometimes struggle to understand what is going on in the world of teenagers? Do you see a beautiful young person one day and then a monster the next? Do you tear your hair out at seemingly inexplicable mood swings? Do you throw up your hands in despair? Do you feel you are losing your relationship with a teenager you genuinely care for?

Welcome to the normal world of the teenager.

The brain, not hormones, is to blame for most of the inexplicable behavior of teenagers.

Mentors do well to pause from time to time and remember their own teenage experiences, how they felt at certain times, and how they responded to situations and different people as they journeyed through confusing times in search of meaning and purpose in their lives.

Some of the more common challenges teenagers face include:

- handling sexually maturing bodies that give rise to strong urges;
- trying, figuring out, and managing volatile and powerful emotions;
- fitting into a complex social network;
- dealing with immense peer pressure;
- dealing with mildly changing moods;
- deciding how to respond to the temptation of tobacco (vaping), alcohol, and drugs;
- figuring out their values;
- renegotiating relationships with their parents or caregivers;
- getting through school, training, or some other form of study;
- figuring out how to have enough sleep (nine hours every night is the preferred option);

- beginning to plan their future.[1]

The plasticity of the brain—it can be changed by experiences—can give *hope* to anyone working with young people. Educator and adolescent brain expert Sheryl Feinstein offers a word of support:

> Promote a sense of mastery in our students. As the brain is naturally social and collaborative, providing opportunities for personal interaction will engage students in the learning process and give them an incentive to keep participating.[2]

The frontal lobes, which make up 40 percent of the brain's total volume, house the "executive" function of the human brain which only stops developing in the mid-twenties. They are the seat of our ability to generate insight, judgment, abstraction, impulse control, and planning. We use this area of the brain to choose a course of action wisely, as the frontal lobes are also the source of self-awareness, and our ability to assess dangers and risks.

Therefore, adolescents need repetition, and to continually learn what responsible choices feel, look, and sound like. When we are not stressed by negative emotions, we can control what information makes it to our brain. In addition, certain activities like interacting with friends, laughing, participating in physical activities, and acting kindly increase the Dopamine—a chemical neurotransmitter—levels in the adolescent brain, which in turn, can boost the young person's learning and ability to process new information. Our brains release *extra* Dopamine when an experience is enjoyable.

Key points from adolescent brain research to help mentors understand the teenage brain

Scientists show that by practicing brain-based skills we can change the way our brains look and operate:

- A positive growth mindset that encourages adolescents to keep working at these skills results in the development of self-confidence—it's a self-empowering journey.

---

1. Walsh, *Why Do They Act That Way?*
2. Feinstein, *Secrets of the Teenage Brain.*

- Training and practice will improve skills *and* change our brains, and build its capacity to use these skills.
- We can provide structures with empowerment, and support young people as they find their voices. Constructive and helpful feedback, at the right time, improves the brain's efficiency.
- People who practice mindfulness on a regular basis have strong coping skills and are resilient in the face of adversity. John Arden states: "Cultivating these skills can help you to rewire your brain."
- The adolescent brain is only 80 percent of the way to maturity. According to neuroscientist Francis Jensen[3] the 20 percent gap is where the wiring is thinnest and this helps explain teenage mood swings, irritability, impulsivity, explosiveness, an inability to focus, follow through and connect with adults, and the temptation to use drugs, alcohol, and engage in other risky behavior. Violent video games, for example, can reinforce violent behavior especially in boys—a reminder of how technology can rewire the brain. Teenagers can overcomplicate problems, idealize the world, and say one thing while doing another.
- As the prefrontal cortex, which is responsible for higher-level cognitive functioning, develops, adolescents begin to climb the moral ladder, yet struggle to see ahead and understand possible consequences of their choices, so they are not really equipped to weigh up the relative harm of risky behavior. This is why access to positive information and experiences is important, as are interactions with parents, teachers, coaches, mentors, and other important adults in their lives. However, they become increasingly capable of moral reasoning and idealism. Sheryl Feinstein states: "They see the world not only as it is, but also how it could be."[4]
- Even though adolescent brains are learning at peak efficiency, much else is inefficient, including attention, self-discipline, task completion, and emotions. Psychologist Karen Young advises:

    > Adolescence is something they have to do on their own. We can guide them, but we can't do it for them. This is their time for growth and learning, but there is something powerful we can do

---

3. Jensen, *The Teenage Brain*.
4. Feinstein, *Secrets of the Teenage Brain*.

to help them along the way. We can give them the information they need to light their way forward.

- Adolescents are not irrational. Their reasoning abilities are likely to be developed by the age of fifteen, so, if they pause and think, they can logically assess if an activity is dangerous or not.
- Studies of the brain clearly show that reflection inward, or in communication with others, stimulates the activation and development of the prefrontal cortex towards its integrative growth—learning to work with both sides of the brain, and growing both sides of the brain.
- Supportive relationships lead to stronger feelings of happiness and healthier lives, while enriched environments stimulate the plasticity of the brain. Teenagers value positive adult influences even though they might complain about it on occasions.
- As adolescents mature, if they know how to keep developing the *positive* skills and activities that release Dopamine, they are less likely to participate in high-risk behaviors like substance abuse, reckless driving, over-eating, inappropriate sexual or antisocial behavior.
- Dopamine, when released in a positive sense, will reinforce goal-directed activity.
- Deficits and excesses of Serotonin—the "take it easy" neurotransmitter—contribute to teenage depression and eating disorders.
- Positive humor boosts the vitality of our thoughts and our emotions, and enhances our ability to deal with stress, anxiety, and depression.
- When adolescents experience a spirit of belonging, they feel happy, and this adds to their social and emotional wellbeing.
- Physical activity can build brain cells, enhance the development of cognitive processing skills, and create strong memory pathways.
- Thinking can be taught, and teenagers crave structure and organization in spite of their attraction to novelty.
- The ability of the brain to rewire and remap itself via neuroplasticity is profound.
- Where a young person grows up in a highly stressful and non-nurturing environment, their brain develops a greater sensitivity to stress and less propensity for healthy, nurturing behavior. They are

more vulnerable to stress than adults, and also have trouble anticipating the consequences of their behavior because they rely more on the emotional amygdala than the rational frontal lobes. The amygdala is the small almond-shaped structure inside the brain, which is part of the larger network of the brain called the limbic system. These are parts of the brain that automatically sense danger.

- Students who believe they have the chance to be successful are intrinsically motivated to learn.
- The brain is naturally social and collaborative.
- ADHD (Attention-Deficit-Hyperactivity Disorder) is not caused by a bad student, bad parent, or bad teacher—the reason can be found in the brain.
- Teenagers who are high in self-control do better in school, have higher self-esteem, better, healthier relationships, and fewer problems with anger.

Sometimes we just need to grit our teeth and speak to the potential we know is within a young person even when they seem unable to see it, possibly even believe it. Persevere. Never quit on any teenager. Every person is beautiful on the inside and the outside. Sometimes it takes a while for them to understand and see this, hence the importance of having a non-judgmental adult cheerleader journeying with our young people during different seasons of adolescence.

Your brain: important features every teenager should know

Most young people are fascinated at the way their brain develops. Here are some key features of the adolescent brain which mentors can share with young people to guide their choices.

- Your brain develops until your mid-twenties, with the frontal lobes (areas) the last to mature—the area of planning, organization, judgment impulse control, and reasoning—so pause and think before choosing to do anything risky. Short-term memory increases by about 30 percent during adolescence.
- Your brain is still developing, so while there are times it will be telling you to "go for it," pause and listen to the voice that might be telling you not to do so—the "voice" will be the correct decision.

UNDERSTAND THE TEENAGE BRAIN

- Your brain reacts to surges of hormones increasing in your body, which can lead to big mood swings. That's normal. Keep communicating with adults you trust, the wise guides walking alongside you, encouraging and supporting you.
- Your brain is still developing and is heavily influenced by whatever you expose it to, positive or negative. This means your brain is extremely vulnerable to stress or *any* type of addiction—it's harder for you to break an addiction than it is for adults—so find adults you trust to encourage and support you.
- Your brain is still developing and so abuse of alcohol might lead to learning difficulties, memory problems, and the risk of other mental health problems. You can choose not to drink alcohol when you are under eighteen (or whatever the legal age is in a particular country).
- Your brain will be fully developed by your mid-twenties so, to keep strengthening and growing it, spend time exploring the things you want to be great at. The activities you invest your time and energy in are likely to influence what activities you invest in as an adult. Never forget that you are unique with special gifts and talents.
- Exercise or physical movement helps the development of your brain, enhances the development of cognitive processing skills, and builds strong memory pathways.
- Your brain releases a feel-good chemical called Dopamine when you get something you want, or even think about some good experiences. Be careful, though, when those thoughts are leading you to do something that's *not* good for you. Your brain is particularly susceptible to novelty, so choose carefully and think about the consequences.
- Your brain is still developing and, therefore, can only focus on *one* thing at a time—be careful about multi-tasking.
- Your brain is still developing and releases a hormone called Melatonin two hours before you sleep (between 7.00 p.m. and 8.00 p.m.), so start slowing down an hour before lights out by reading, listening to music, relaxing away from a computer, or TV, or activity on a cellphone. Melatonin changes your sleep patterns.
- Your brain is still developing and there is an increase in the "bonding hormone," Oxytocin, which will make you more self-conscious as you start thinking about who you want to be and your place in the world,

so allow adults you trust to journey with you—they were teenagers once.

- Your brain is still developing and it's normal that you are ruled far more by your emotions than by logic. In other words, there will be times when you experience emotions *before* you can verbally express them.
- Your education, work experiences, family, friends, and other life experiences are shaping your thoughts and choices.

Brain research highlights that our learning power increases when we pursue activities that give us a sense of accomplishment. Never stop developing strategies to inspire a young person to achieve greatness or to reach their unique potential.

Reflection

The development of neuroimaging (brain scanning) technologies such as positron emissions topography (PET) and functional magnetic resonance imaging technologies (fMRI) now allow researchers to peer inside the skulls of people who are alive without using a scalpel. As a result, new insights about how the brain and the mind develop, their role in the body, and how this works occur almost daily.

—Jeannette Vos[5]

---

5. Vos, *The Learning Revolution 2.0*.

8. Ten mentoring life lessons my students taught me

What is the greatest life lesson a young person has taught you? Can you remember the actual time and place where that occurred?

There are more than ten mentoring life lessons my students taught me over the years. However, these are the most important and, as I have reflected on them, I appreciate how important these are for anyone who invests their time and energy to mentor young people.

A student like Lucas, for example, probably has no idea how a brief conversation with me transformed my life, and made my interactions with other students more meaningful. Are you teachable? Lucas, for example, sowed the seeds of the spirit of mentoring in my life early in my teaching career. Let me begin with that example, as I share the ten mentoring lessons my students taught me.

1. *Be authentic.* Sixteen-year-old Lucas was my first team hockey captain in the late 1970s. After a practice we stood on the side of the field chatting. I rested one foot on a short picket fence. "Sir, we don't know whether you are being serious or not," Lucas said to me. At the time I had a strange, cynical sense of humor. I realized, on reflection, that it had become a defensive mechanism I had created while I was recovering from cancer as a teenager. Lucas' statement hit me between the eyes. I apologized for the added confusion I was causing young lives whose brains were experiencing significant development. The journey to be true to myself began that day and continues all these years later. Trust, empathy, integrity, and respect are solid foundations on which mentoring relationships can be built. Bobb Biehl suggested that a person's character, commitment, and love ultimately determines

SECTION ONE: THE ROLE OF A MENTOR

the effectiveness of the mentoring process, not a person's style, or skills, or temperament.

2. *Be empathetic.* I have no idea how many times a young person has asked me if I was listening to them—not simply hearing them, actually *listening* to their opinions, ideas, dreams, and doing my best to *connect* with their feelings. These young people taught me the importance of making every effort to walk in their shoes for a while, and sometimes to feel the blisters—the depth of their pain; how they are seeing themselves so I might better understand their priorities in life. As I developed my communication skills, I learnt how to look behind the mask and communicate at a deeper level, because effective communication techniques produce mentoring from the heart.

3. *Know your subject.* Students are incredibly perceptive. Every student knows when a teacher has not prepared a lesson. I prided myself on the depth of my lesson preparation, and was always quick to acknowledge if I did not know the answer to a question. The answer would be found, either in collaboration with the students, or before our next lesson. Young people who risk developing meaningful relationships with adults, often seek more knowledge, and wish to tap into the wisdom of someone they admire and respect. My students encouraged me to write a book which has been shared with many young people over the years: *Letter 2 a Teen—Become the Best I can Be.* Mentors are valued as key resources by mentees, especially when they link their mentees to personal networks.

4. *Be respectful.* My students continually taught me the importance of respecting them as unique individuals with their own gifts and talents. This included a genuine respect for their ideas and opinions, as well as respect for the specific challenges they might have been dealing with at any particular time. Of course, I made many mistakes on this career journey. Many students sincerely appreciated my non-judgmental cheerleading during a season of their lives as this respect was developed. I learnt that I should not expect to have all the answers. Mentors are, after all, human beings who are not expected to be perfect.

5. *Have a sense of humor.* Students love a teacher (mentor) who has a great sense of humor and can laugh at themselves, as students will inevitably play pranks on their teachers to test them. I have always

had a great sense of humor—one of my strengths. My students helped refine and shape my sense of humor (thank you, Lucas) and, often through our interactions, reminded me that I needed to remember what life was like when I was a teenager, and what amused my child-like mind at the time. In turn, as I modeled a sense of humor, I was able to coach students how to laugh at themselves, such an important life skill.

6. *Acknowledge effort above performance.* There were many times students could show me all the work they had done, even when their final assessment might not have made the grade. They taught me how important it was to affirm their *efforts*. This strategy inevitably would lead to a lift in their performance. I also learnt to speak to the potential of a student who could not see that potential for any number of reasons at the time.

7. *Be fair.* Every teacher will probably experience accusations from students that they favor some students over others. My students challenged me about this early in my career. Thereafter, I automatically became the champion of the underdog—probably because of my personal challenges as a teenager, and how I learnt to deal with the impact of those experiences on my life—and did my best never to have favorites. Of course, some students will say I failed dismally in this area. Students continually reminded me of the importance of being fair at all times and how much they valued this—a great life lesson, as often the discussion would move to a chat about how to resolve conflicts positively, yet another wonderful life lesson for us all.

8. *Be on time.* Students seldom rush to find their teacher when the latter is late for class, yet they appreciate a teacher who is either punctual or standing at the door to welcome them to the new class. There were two life lessons my students taught me about the effective management of time. Firstly, they raised their level of academic performance when I returned work promptly, efficiently, and commented constructively on their effort. My comment was personal, in that it was addressed directly to the student using their first name. Secondly, they respected and valued my investment in their lives when I showed my care and compassion, and arranged extra time to meet with them outside of the normal class time. Our collaborative life lesson involved learning how and when to apologize—when I was late, or missed a deadline. This, in turn, became a life lesson about how and when to be vulnerable.

9. *Play to win.* I have always been a competitive person who does not like to lose. Over the years, students taught me how to lose graciously, while never accepting a half-hearted effort. Discussions would focus on the importance of every choice we make, and the development of teamwork, courage, and perseverance. My teaching and coaching skills were sharpened by these positive interactions.

10. *Be a positive cheerleader.* I learnt the importance of celebrating the small victories with the students with whom I interacted inside and outside the classroom, and how much they valued these moments. I became a positive cheerleader in the lives of many young people, helping and encouraging them to achieve their personal, realistic goals on their journey to reach their potential—possibly for only one season of their lives. Mentors can look for every opportunity to acknowledge their mentees' *efforts* rather than focus on performance.

My interactions with students fine-tuned my leadership skills, and remain a continual reminder that my life purpose is to serve others no matter what the personal cost might be. Challenging, for sure, though immensely rewarding and satisfying.

I celebrate all the students who have welcomed me into their lives and taught me so much, and I recall a supportive mentoring strategy shared by mentoring expert Ross McCook: "The greatest driver of personal development is the commitment to the personal development of someone else."[1]

How about you? What five life lessons have your interactions with young people taught you?

Reflection

Your role as a mentor becomes a knowledgeable navigator, a non-judgmental sounding board and a partner whose goal is to affirm, support, and encourage. This is the foundation to developing young people who have confidence in their voice and can affect positive change in our society.

—ELIZABETH SANTIAGO AND MINNIE CHEN[2]

---

1. McCook, *Heart for Youth.*
2. Santiago and Chen, *Becoming a Better Mentor.*

9. How my *ideal* teacher models and promotes the spirit of mentoring

Can you think of a teacher who had a positive impact on your life? Have you ever thought what your ideal teacher would be like? These are good questions to ask a young person, as their answers will provide some insights into their thinking.

As I watch my grandchildren playing with their friends, and listen to others talking about the concerns they have about education, I find myself reflecting back to my childhood and the teachers who significantly impacted my life journey. How privileged I was, as all these people displayed aspects of the spirit of mentoring.

I appreciate even more that most adults are parents, or teachers, or coaches, or mentors—in reality, a combination of these. In other words, whether we like it or not, we will either positively or negatively impact the young people with whom we interact. Retired school principal Graham Coyle writes: "If teaching is about anything, it is about helping people into what is currently beyond them,"[1] a comment that would equally apply to the mentoring journey.

Positive traits of my *ideal* teacher

- affirms life and furthers its potential, and always shares messages of hope;
- enters into real discussions with their students because, at heart, they are youth driven, genuine, and emotionally available. Jeannette Vos offers a supportive thought:

1. Coyle, *To Infinity*.

As adults, if we can keep a child-like sense of wonder and awe, we learn best naturally. When we allow ourselves to think freely, share our thoughts, and act on them together, we change how the world learns, thinks and behaves. We have the cognitive ability to achieve a life of learning every time we decide. Every decision counts. We have learned that—often the hard way.[2]

- respects and sets clear boundaries—usually *negotiated* with older students—for themselves and others;
- embodies values and virtues that others merely admire; walks the talk;

Our values make up our basic belief system about what is good or bad, right or wrong, and what makes life meaningful and worth living. These general principles are fundamentally important to us as individuals. They are likely to greatly affect our attitudes and opinions, and our decisions in key areas such as education, career possibilities, friends, and good relationships.[3]

- always makes sure their students feel safe and secure in their company;
- looks to identify their students' strengths, names them, and encourages these young people to use these strengths in positive ways to master the art of self-learning—preferably with the support of a trusted adult—and the development of resiliency;
- possesses a great sense of humor, is able to laugh at themselves, and creates a fun learning environment;
- creates a nurturing and trusting environment. Demonstrates trust in the students they influence, by being:
  - authentic, rather than putting on an act or being phony—their goals are aligned with their values and feelings;
  - consistent;
  - compassionate and caring;
  - sensitive to differences;
  - a positive, non-judgmental cheerleader;
  - a good listener;

---

2. Vos, *The Learning Revolution 2.0.*
3. Cox, *The Mentoring Spirit*, 39.

- humble, empathetic, and promoting understanding with everyone with whom they interact. The focus of their relationship with their students is always on the latter's goals, needs, and their lives;
- are organized, and respectfully models and guides students to become better organized as they chase their dreams. Discusses the effective management of time, with a focus on living a healthy and balanced lifestyle;
- coaches goal setting in a fun and achievable way, and encourages the development of innovative, creative, and entrepreneurial thinking;
- *never* quits on their students; continually explores different ways to encourage students to reach their potential; speaks to the potential many students often do not see; reaches out a helping hand to a student who stumbles and falls, and places them back on the "dream path" with a gentle pat on the back, and a reminder not to quit;
- promotes a sense of unity in their students' lives—family unity, the importance of teamwork, learning how to positively resolve conflicts, and building community.

Of course, much more can be written about an ideal teacher. Your story will be different from mine. Your needs as a student were probably different from mine, although as teenagers we all wanted to be loved and cared for, to feel valued, and to know that our lives had meaning and purpose.

I celebrate the many teachers who put up with my mischievous nonsense, or cheek, laughed lots, guided me through challenging times, spoke to the potential I often could not see, and embraced most of the ideals shared above.

My history teacher, Philip LeFeuvre, was one of those influential adults in my fourteen-year-old life, whose teaching style impacted me in a powerful way, and reinforced my desire to become a teacher.

I managed to track down Philip, now in his 80s and retired, to thank him for the impact he had on my life all those years ago.

Philip responded to my letter—a message of encouragement for all who mentor or coach young people, perhaps:

> Thank you so much for writing that letter. We seek to fill our days with that which is good and productive and worthwhile, but do not really know just what we have achieved in the lives of others,

or what we have left behind us. But we know that God knows and that it is almost certain that He has taken what we have offered and made it far more than we could ever imagine. Your letter, for which I am immensely thankful, confirms that for me and encourages me in the involvement of all that lies ahead.

I wonder what your *ideal* teacher would be like? Remember to look in the mirror from time to time, smile, and remind yourself to be the teacher—or mentor—you would like to have had in your interactions with young people, and you will promote the spirit of mentoring.

Reflection

For people to grow and flourish they also need a climate of hope. Ideally schools can provide these climates of hope and teachers are crucial in this ... When we cultivate a climate of hopefulness, we begin to change the way our pupils perceive themselves and their futures.

—Graham Coyle[4]

---

4. Coyle, *To Infinity*.

SECTION TWO

Strategies and tips to inspire and build meaningful relationships with young people

This section offers hundreds of strategies and tips to support anyone working with young people to make a quick connection, and begin the process of building meaningful relationships with them. Some helpful strategies and tips about the responsible use of social media are included, along with supportive tips and strategies mentors can encourage their mentees to share with their peers as they strive to reach their unique potential.

… an extensive body of research has linked a young person's goal-directed skills to healthy and positive development as well as making positive contributions to their communities. Higher levels of goal-directed skills are also linked with lower levels of depressive symptoms, delinquency, and risky behaviors such as smoking, underage drinking and substance abuse.

—ED BOWERS[1]

1. Bowers, *Becoming a Better Mentor.*

1. Fun ideas for the mentoring journey

Marc Freedman comments that, "in addition to providing a sympathetic ear, mentors supply affiliation and security for youth. They can also help them have fun, an aspect which can't be overestimated, given the deplorable quality of life so many face."[1]

Fun ideas could have a positive effect on the communication between a mentor and a mentee. Here are some key points that may influence that communication process:

- we are unique *individuals*; each of us differs from all the others. We come from different families, and possibly different ethnic backgrounds and cultures, and we have different personal experiences;
- we differ in the things we want from life and each other;
- we differ in our dreams, wishes, and expectations.

Our uniqueness means that two individuals may respond in different ways to the same situation. This potentially complicates communication greatly. Communication can be difficult to the extent that the two people (or groups of people) communicating differ in values, perceptions, and/or assumptions.

The choice of activities will naturally depend on the age of the mentee, and the setting of their mentoring relationship. The variety of activities in the lists that follow should offer something of interest for most ages, and hopefully stimulate a mentor's thinking for more positive ways in which they can spend time together. A great mentor always asks their mentee for ideas once they have established a positive connection in a mentoring atmosphere that is, in the words of Samuel McQuillin, "characterized by compassion, acceptance and empathy,"[2] and in which the young person feels safe and secure.

1. Freedman, *The Kindness*, 69.
2. McQuillin, *Becoming a Better Mentor.*

SECTION TWO: STRATEGIES AND TIPS TO INSPIRE

The fun ideas are divided into five lists:

i. Community and general fun ideas
ii. "Go to" fun ideas
iii. School and study fun ideas
iv. Fitness and exercise fun ideas
v. Life skills fun ideas

i. Community and general fun ideas

1. Visit a car museum.
2. Visit a major harbor (where applicable).
3. Play computer games or X-Box—Nintendo or Play Station.
4. Visit the SPCA or another animal shelter.
5. Visit an art gallery.
6. Listen to your favorite music together.
7. Visit your old school and share your story.
8. Visit your mentee's school and let them show you around.
9. Entertain a sick child or sick children in hospital.
10. Visit an old age home, and entertain the elderly, play games with them, and listen to their life stories.
11. Talk about how to form meaningful relationships—it is helpful if the mentor facilitates a role-play of a possible discussion between a mentee and their friend, or relative.
12. Draw your family tree and talk about your respective cultural beliefs. Your mentee might want to explore their family tree, though this should not be forced on them.
13. Visit an armed service, naval, or air force base.
14. Write a song or piece of music together.
15. Do good deeds for three strangers together.
16. Enjoy a picnic at a nearby lake, zoo, park, beach, or mountain.
17. Prepare a surprise party for the mentor program coordinator (where relevant).

FUN IDEAS FOR THE MENTORING JOURNEY

18. "Surf the net" together and discuss how it can be used responsibly—choose a research topic.
19. Fly a kite.
20. Watch an age-appropriate movie and then discuss it.
21. Play board games, chess, or cards.
22. Play charades.
23. Mow lawns together.
24. Watch and discuss the TV news.
25. Audition for a drama production or a choral event together.
26. Spend time together taking photographs, discussing photography, or making a short video.
27. Create a journal, and include photos of your time together.
28. Start a collection—for example, stamps or coins, shells or rocks, sport cards, insects or whatever else is the craze at the time.
29. Visit important statues in the city and talk about the city and country's history.
30. Arrange a visit for your mentee to visit their hero (where possible).
31. Visit a local radio or media station.
32. Arrange a clothes collection with other mentors and mentees for a charity of your choice.
33. Arrange a treasure hunt or an Easter egg hunt for some children in foster care.
34. Participate in World Vision's 40-hour Fast (or a similar service project) as a joint project, and challenge other mentors and mentees to participate. Finish with a celebration.
35. Visit the home of a potter and attempt to make something.
36. Begin a book club or music club with other mentors and mentees.
37. Visit Parliament or a local Council meeting.
38. Help out at a local faith or charity shop, or thrift store.
39. Arrange a garage sale with other mentors and mentees, and donate the proceeds to a children's charity.

40. Offer to help serve meals to the homeless, or to help out at a shelter for needy people (as appropriate).
41. Adopt an elderly neighbor and carry out some chores for them, or go and visit from time to time.
42. Organize a recycling project with other mentors and mentees.
43. During winter arrange a collection of blankets through the school or a community club for the hungry and homeless.
44. Have lunch together once a week (where possible).
45. Do a jigsaw puzzle together.
46. Take a walk around the neighborhood and talk about being a responsible citizen—collect litter while you walk and talk.
47. Clean out the garage together and then celebrate a job well done.
48. Invite your mentee to "job shadow" you for a day during the school holidays.
49. Join a community environmental project—plant trees.
50. Bake a cake and deliver it to your local police or fire station.
51. Volunteer to be trained as life guards at your local beach or pool.
52. Volunteer to facilitate a collection of used glasses (eye glasses), including sun glasses, for donation to an organization that collects, cleans, repairs, and distributes them to people in need.
53. Play Dodgem Cars (where available).
54. Play petanque, or carpet bowls, or darts.
55. Visit a circus.
56. Visit paintball and have some fun.
57. Feed the ducks or eels (whatever is appropriate).

Reflection

Every person is a teacher and a learner. The young people in your life are sources of knowledge, skills, and information that can be greatly beneficial in your own growth. Take the time to both teach and learn, investing in a bidirectional relationship. Allowing youth to "give back" in this way can be a gift to you both!

—CARLA HERRERA AND MICHAEL GARRINGER[3]

3. Herrera and Garringer, *Becoming a Better Mentor.*

ii. "Go to" fun ideas

1. Go to a movie.
2. Go to a concert.
3. Go to the library.
4. Go to a theatre.
5. Go to the swimming pools or hot spring.
6. Go to the beach.
7. Go to the gym.
8. Go to a community Fair or similar event.
9. Go to an indoor climbing wall.
10. Go to the War Memorial or some other local museum.
11. Go to the weekend markets.
12. Go to a sports game.
13. Go to a bargain hunting event.
14. Go to a church or faith institution.
15. Go to a horse show.
16. Go to a motor car or motorbike race.
17. Go to a cultural festival.
18. Go to a War Remembrance (or similar remembrance) gathering, and discuss the impact of wars and violence in the world.
19. Go to a fun outdoor event of your mentee's choice.
20. Go to your place of work together—check out your workplace's website (where applicable).

Reflection

Mentoring is just plain fun. You take your mentee to the movies, out to dinner, to a ball game. You share what you know about the world, your interests, your enthusiasms. You get to see life through the eyes of a child, pick up new words, hear new music. You breathe in the vitality of youth and the satisfaction of bringing another person along.

—Thomas Dortch Jr.[4]

4. Dortch, *The Miracles of Mentoring*.

iii. School and study fun ideas

Most young people find it helpful when I share my goal setting experiences with them; how I had to adapt goals to changing circumstances; how my short-term goals were linked to my long-term goals using a helpful strategy offered by mentoring expert Ross McCook: "Is my *here and now* able to take me *there and then*?"[5]

Graham Coyle reminds us of the importance of being the positive role model during this journey: "If we want to release the power of dreaming and imagination into others, it needs to operate in us first …"[6]

1. Set your mentoring goals together.
2. Help your mentee with some homework or a research project.
3. Talk about how to plan a career.
4. Get together with friends from work to share career stories.
5. Take tours of friends' places of work.
6. Visit a tertiary institution Open Day.
7. Work on a resume.
8. Do a credible personality test (online).
9. Help your mentee set academic and other school goals.
10. Do a pretend job interview.
11. Discuss what to do in an emergency; who to call, and what the process is.
12. Help your mentee develop public speaking skills.
13. Talk about how to find and attain a suitable job, or how to find a part-time job.
14. Set up a work experience opportunity.
15. Talk about balancing work and play, and having a healthy diet.
16. Talk about any after-school activities that may interest your mentee.
17. Talk about personal values.

---

5. McCook, *Heart for Youth*.
6. Coyle, *To Infinity*.

18. Talk about the future—life in general—and discuss your mentee's hopes and fears.
19. Talk about the effective management of time.
20. Review your mentoring goals together every three months.
21. Ask your mentee for honest feedback about your role as a mentor. What is working well? What needs to improve? Suggestions?
22. Coach your mentee how to use a paper diary, or phone calendar, or online "notepad" effectively.

Reflection

When we get discouraged in our work with people, it is important to draw back and remind ourselves that there is no more noble occupation in the world than to assist another human being to help someone else succeed.
—ALAN MCGINNIS

iv. Fitness and exercise fun ideas

A huge factor in determining a great life full of satisfying and meaningful relationships, worthy achievements, and simply the ability to push through life successfully, is the way in which we see *ourselves*. Sadly, many of us [of all ages] spend more time bound up in what we think *others* think of us, rather than valuing what we think of ourselves.
—ROSS MCCOOK[7]

A mentor's aim is to contribute to the development of the *whole* person.

Remember that most young people are searching for identity and self-esteem. They want people to respect them as unique individuals. Their request is simple: "Give me the chance to be me and not somebody else." Often, they are unable to verbalize this clearly. When mentors undertake fun activities with young people, it is amazing how these activities can

---

7. McCook, *Heart for Youth*.

SECTION TWO: STRATEGIES AND TIPS TO INSPIRE

result in transformative discussions as the young person relaxes and enjoys the activity in a non-threatening environment.

1. Participate in a fun run or walk event.
2. Go roller-skating, rollerblading, or play roller-hockey.
3. Form a group and go Ten Pin Bowling.
4. Play a sport together—basketball, netball, golf, badminton, table tennis, tennis, pickleball, or squash racquets.
5. Go hiking, kayaking, camping, or sailing.
6. Go to a skateboard park. Use the experience of learning to skateboard to coach goal setting.
7. Go fishing.
8. Go bird watching.
9. Go on nature walks.
10. Play with a frisbee or participate in some other fun outdoor game like mini-golf.
11. Play snooker or pool together.
12. Go ice skating.
13. Coach younger children a sport skill.
14. Go hunting.
15. Go skiing.
16. Go tubing.
17. Go cycling.
18. Go jogging.
19. Go snorkeling together.
20. Go and watch a club sport together. This could motivate your mentee to pursue a sport, or join the club.
21. Help your mentee draw up a fitness schedule.
22. Do aerobics together.

Reflection

Exercise that elevates your heart rate is a great way to overcome stress, create a happier mood, fight memory loss and best of all, create a sharper intellect for peak performance.

—Jeannette Vos[8]

v. Life skills fun ideas

Elizabeth Santiago and Minie Chen note that, "the mentoring relationship may be one of the few places a young person can be their authentic self with an adult. We want them to feel safe, and be accepted for who they are."[9] As this relationship develops, and the young person feels supported, research highlights some examples of what young people receive:

- increased feelings of self-worth;
- a sense of belonging;
- a better perspective on themselves;
- a feeling of significance;
- a sense of hope about who they can become.

Here are some life skills and fun ideas to enhance and deepen the connection between a mentor and a young person:

1. Make dinner (or a meal) together.
2. Go out for a meal together—discuss responsible behavior in a restaurant, or public place.
3. Make popcorn and talk.
4. Pick fruit.
5. Discuss the responsible use of a cellphone (technology), and how to handle cyberbullying (text bullying) in a responsible way—talk about the strength of asking for help.
6. Sew on a button.

---

8. Vos, *Self-Learning: The Future*.
9. Santiago and Chen, *Becoming a Better Mentor*.

SECTION TWO: STRATEGIES AND TIPS TO INSPIRE

7. Take photos or videos of favorite people or places.
8. Change a car tire or a bicycle tire.
9. Make fish hooks or flies.
10. Open a bank account or some other savings account.
11. Talk about credit cards, and the responsible use of credit cards.
12. Talk about budgeting.
13. Plan a week's worth of meals.
14. Do a week's grocery shopping (where appropriate).
15. Write "thank you" notes.
16. Make puppets and put on a show for friends.
17. Take a ferry ride.
18. Take a train ride together.
19. Go on a bus trip.
20. Do dancing lessons, or create a dance.
21. Have some fun with face painting, or visit a children's home and do some face painting there.
22. Show your mentee how to read a map, or use a compass.
23. Show your mentee how to use an answer phone.
24. Discuss how to write and respond to emails or messages in a responsible way. Chat about developing positive life skills, like the habit of responding to messages or emails within twenty-four hours of receiving them, even if it is just an acknowledgment that the email or message has been received.
25. Open a library membership together.
26. Learn how a car operates—do a basic maintenance course together.
27. Participate in woodwork or carpentry activities.
28. Wash and clean a car together. Use the opportunity to discuss similarities between the process of car washing and looking after their wellbeing, or being proud of who they are, their appearance, and how they present themselves on different occasions, or at different events—formal or informal.

FUN IDEAS FOR THE MENTORING JOURNEY

29. Discuss the importance of networking.
30. Play Sudoku.
31. Talk about taxes.
32. Discuss how to program a DVD, or develop an app, or download an app.
33. Design a website home page.
34. Visit an airport and look at all aspects: ticketing; reading a monitor or travel schedule; checking in; going through security.
35. Build, create, or design something—even using Lego or Meccano.
36. Make a picture frame, a birthday or Christmas card, or a card for a special occasion, or a bird feeding tray for the garden.
37. Paint something.
38. Create a business card (and logo) together for your mentee's imaginary business.
39. Fix an appliance.
40. Plant and maintain a vegetable garden.
41. Visit a local nursery. Purchase a tree or plant which you plant together, and observe its growth during the months ahead.
42. Visit an aquarium and talk about responsible use of the environment, and the different opinions about climate change.
43. Do needlework such as knitting or embroidery.
44. Look for suitable accommodation together (where applicable).
45. Visit a travel agent—look at brochures and then try and organize an overseas travel trip. This is also a great activity to discuss goal setting—developing an itinerary; understanding how an airline pilot must know where they are going before they board the airplane, and how to plan for a trip.
46. Build a model car or airplane together.
47. Design a house, or school, or community playground—encourage innovative and creative thinking.
48. Do clay modeling.
49. Create your own board game together.

SECTION TWO: STRATEGIES AND TIPS TO INSPIRE

50. Learn how to make origami.
51. Visit a car yard together.
52. Make a variety of paper airplanes.
53. Visit a farm and talk to the farmer about farming life.
54. Visit the local courthouse; attend a court hearing (where age-appropriate).
55. Do an age-appropriate crossword puzzle, or design one.
56. Ask your mentee to teach you something which they are good at or enjoy.
57. Do some baking or craft making which you can sell at the local market—an opportunity to explore budgeting, and how to set up a small business.

Reflection

Only those who dare to fail greatly can ever achieve greatly.
—Robert F. Kennedy

2. Discussion topics to build meaningful mentoring relationships

Encourage young people to be young. Comprehend the cultural context of the young person: read their magazines, watch some of their favorite TV shows and movies; talk to them about their experiences and challenges. Constantly reinterpret events and experiences to perceive the meaning of life through a teenager. Keep the focus on the child, *not* the adult. Admit mistakes or lack of understanding. Commit time to get to know the teen, to share experiences and create a deeper relationship; prepare to be vulnerable; stand beside your mentee through their darkest hours—telephone, text, email, postcards; engage them in the learning process. Teens absorb principles and values best when they have the chance to participate in developing a deeply-rooted comprehension and application of those elements.

—[ADAPTED] GEORGE BARNA[1]

We know from our personal life experiences how long it takes to build trusting relationships with others. When two strangers meet for the first time from different backgrounds, cultures, ethnicities, life experiences, and of different ages, this becomes a challenging, yet incredibly rewarding journey when the connection is made, and the trust established.

When mentees develop good communication skills, they enhance their self-confidence, and develop meaningful relationships with others. Effective or active listening lies at the very heart of mentoring. Mentees who are listened to are likely to:

1. Barna, *Real Teens*.

- feel accepted as young people;
- feel good about the mentor (the listener);
- become clearer about what is on their minds;
- think better about possible solutions;
- feel less anxious (if they had been anxious);
- receive a complete and accurate message.

Effective communication techniques are all about adopting communication methods that will help mentees to talk, and to share their feelings and experiences.

Five Levels of communication

Some research suggests that there are five levels of communication that move mentors from surface responses to ultimate sharing and connection with their mentees:

Level 1: *clichés*—How was school today?

Level 2: *facts*—Which film did you see?

Level 3: *ideas*—What do you think about that CD or YouTube clip? Which was your favorite track on that CD and why?

Level 4: *feelings*—How did you feel when you failed to score in the match on Saturday?

Level 5: *intimate sharing*—What was on your heart when your mum and dad were disagreeing again the other night?

Moving to Levels 4 and 5 takes time. Many mentors might only get to Level 3 or 4, depending on the length of the mentoring relationship, and that is okay.

Here are more suggestions to help build rapport and connect with young people. As with any friendship or meaningful relationship, once the trust is developed, it is possible to communicate at a deeper level. Be patient. Be kind to yourself, and display a positive and empathetic attitude as you connect with any young person.

There will be repetition in some questions. Other questions might not be suitable for the age group you teach, mentor, coach, or guide. Use wisdom and discernment when choosing a topic, and do your best to ask open-ended questions. Most questions will lead to different doors for communication opening. Be prepared for this. It is worthwhile to keep a journal of topics discussed during the mentoring journey where this is possible.

These discussion topics, which are divided into five groups, have been gathered from a variety of resources over many years. Many, for example, could be used during the early stages of the mentoring relationship. I salute and express my gratitude to all who have shared these topics.[2]

i. Key questions

ii. General questions

iii. Questions: Feelings, Friendships, and Experiences

iv. More general questions

v. Questions: deeper topics

i. Key questions

These key questions can often be valuable to unlock the relationship, and encourage your mentee to feel safe and secure.

1. What are your expectations of this mentoring experience?
2. What role would you like me to play as your mentor?
3. In what ways can I help, support, or encourage you?
4. How comfortable are you using a camera with online communication?
5. Where have you come from? What is your life history to this point (only share what you are comfortable sharing)?
6. Who are the adults who support you best?
7. Which friends do you enjoy hanging around with?
8. Share *any* three things you have done in recent weeks which made you feel proud. I'll share three things I have done, if you would like me to do so.
9. Describe your perfect day to me.

---

2. Cox, *CHOICES*, 149-161.

10. How comfortable are you using different social media platforms? Any in particular you are more comfortable, or uncomfortable with?

11. What has been *one* highlight for you during the past week? (This question can open the door to many discussions.)

Reflection

Always celebrate your mentees' successes, both big and small ... all ways!
—Ross McCook[3]

ii. General questions

An unknown author wrote these encouraging words:

> Ensuring the sustained presence of a caring adult in a young person's life is especially critical during adolescence ... [when] students face serious decisions about which courses they will take, what activities they will engage in, and how seriously they will take their school work. For the most at-risk youths, the presence of an adult mentor can be essential for reinforcing the importance of school, fostering good work habits and study skills, and providing youths with the information they need to make the right choices.[4]

Through asking some general questions, a mentor expresses a message of support and care, a respect for the young person's opinions and ideas, and a genuine interest in that young life.

1. Describe a practical joke one day at school.
2. Describe a teacher or coach who has made a big impression on you (either positive or negative).
3. Describe a time when a message or conversation radically impacted or transformed your life?
4. Who is one of the most unforgettable people you have met? Why this person?

---

3. McCook, *Heart for Youth*.
4. Cox, *Mentoring Minutes*, 73.

TOPICS TO BUILD MEANINGFUL MENTORING RELATIONSHIPS

5. Share a recent situation or occasion where you were instrumental in the growth of another person. What did you do or say?
6. If there was one person in the world (living or dead) that you could spend a day with, who would this be? Why?
7. If you could choose to go anywhere in the world for ten days, where would you go? What would you do? Why this place?
8. What was a gift that you received from someone that really meant a lot to you?
9. When you were younger, who was the neighborhood bully, or the bully in your community? What made that person so frightening? How did you deal with them, or respond to the situation?
10. Who was your hero when you were growing up? Or, who is your hero today? What made that person, or those people special?
11. If you could go on national television and warn people to avoid three things, what would you say?
12. If you could invite anyone to join you for a meal, who would you ask? Why?
13. If your house was on fire, what three items (not people or pets) would you try and save?
14. What one little thing really bugs, or annoys, or irritates you? Why?
15. If you could have one of the following superpowers, which one would you choose: the ability to fly? Super strength? Able to become invisible? Why did you choose this power?
16. If you were trapped on a deserted island, and could pick one famous person (living or dead) to join you, who would you choose? Why?
17. Who are two or three great musicians you admire? Why these people?
18. Which TV or movie star do your friends think is amazing, yet you do not share the same feelings? Why is this?
19. What is one of the great memories you have from your time spent with your family during the past two or three years?
20. What are your favorite movies? Violence? Travel? Adventure? Comedy? Romance? Science-fiction? Is there one favorite movie you have watched a number of times?

SECTION TWO: STRATEGIES AND TIPS TO INSPIRE

21. Imagine you were given a free ticket to visit any place in the world. Where would you visit and why?
22. People talk about heaven and earth. Do you believe in heaven? If so, what do you think it is like? Alternatively, what do you believe?
23. What is the most terrifying or scariest movie you have ever watched? Why?
24. Much has been written about how much TV time or computer time should be allowed each day. If you were a parent, what would you say to your children (who are now your age)?
25. Imagine you are alone in a deserted area. Someone from outer space arrives who can speak your language. You are not frightened. What would you talk about?
26. What is the funniest movie you have ever seen? What happened?
27. You can choose your favorite pizza. What two or three flavors would you choose? Ice-cream to follow—your two or three favorite flavors? Oh, there is a soft drink too. Your choice?
28. Have you been on any memorable beach walks, or tramps, or special hikes? Maybe a school or some other youth group camping experience? What walks would you like to do if you had a free choice? Is there something local we could do together, or with a friend and their mentor?
29. If you could choose any three people to be your mentors or non-judgmental cheerleaders, who would they be? Why these people?
30. What book are you reading at the moment? (A mentor can share the books they read as a teenager, and a book they are reading during the mentoring journey.)
31. Who in your family or extended family can you turn to for support?
32. Describe your toughest life experience to date? How did you get through it? What did you learn about yourself from the experience? (A strategic tip for a mentor: Can you identify and name one strength as your mentee shares? This could be a life-changing moment, which also builds resiliency.)
33. Tell me about the most interesting person you have met to date. Why was that person so interesting?

34. Shall we share our most memorable holiday experiences?
35. What do you see as the main problems or issues facing young people in your community? What can you and your friends, or you and I do to improve the situation?
36. If you were given the opportunity to spend four weeks wherever you liked, all expenses paid, where would you go? Why?
37. What is your favorite food? Can you cook or bake? How about we teach one another a favorite recipe, maybe even cook a meal for your parents, or caregivers, or some friends?
38. What is your favorite dessert?
39. What is your favorite school or work lunch? Who do you eat lunch with at school, or in the workplace (whichever is relevant)?
40. What are your favorite magazines—either online or paper copies? Why these choices?
41. What is your favorite boardgame?
42. What is your favorite card game?

Reflection

…we should help young people critically interrogate their world by having open and honest conversations with them, and providing them with varied perspectives. Instead of presenting them with what we think, we should present them with the possibilities and let them choose. … Just remember that they should be in the lead and your role is as a coconspirator helping to bring their vision to life.

—Tori Weiston-Serdan[5]

iii. Questions: Feelings, Friendships, and Experiences

The following quotes have inspired me during my mentoring role. They remind me of the importance of an empathetic attitude, especially relevant in the questions that follow.

5. Weiston-Serdan, *Becoming a Better Mentor.*

SECTION TWO: STRATEGIES AND TIPS TO INSPIRE

Learn to be a comforter. Stand with people in their pain. Walk with them in their adversity. Weep with them in their suffering. Share your own pain. Be real. And most of all, be short on words and long on service.
—David Stoddard[6]

Treat a man as he appears to be, and you make him worse. But treat a man as if he already were what he potentially could be, and you make him what he should be.
—Johann Wolfgang Von Goethe

Some people come into our lives and quickly go. Some stay for a while and leave footprints on our hearts. And we are never, ever the same.
—Flavia Weedn

1. Who are you angry with right now? Why?
2. If someone asks you: "What does it mean to care for someone?", how would you respond?
3. How easily do you forgive a friend who lets you down? Can you share a recent experience with me?
4. How old were you when you first realized that one day you would die? What caused you to think about death?
5. If you could change two things about the way you were raised, what would they be? If you come from a divorced family, how does it affect you?
6. What type of music do you enjoy listening to? Why?
7. Which do you value most: sight, or hearing, or speech? Why?
8. If you could wake up tomorrow morning having gained one quality or ability, what would it be?
9. What one thing have you learned about yourself during the mentoring journey, or during our time together?
10. How would you respond to this statement? "Today, what I would like to change about myself is … because …"

---

6. Stoddard, *The Heart*.

TOPICS TO BUILD MEANINGFUL MENTORING RELATIONSHIPS

11. Under what circumstances do you feel most lonely? Least lonely? Why?
12. What is one of your biggest fears of the future? Why?
13. What is the first thing that comes to mind when you think about God?
14. Who is your closest friend today? Why this person? (Maybe there is more than one person.)
15. Describe your "ideal" teacher?
16. How important is your privacy to you? When do you prefer to be alone? Why?
17. What do you do when you are feeling sad? What cheers you up? Is there a special meal you would like at such times, or something else?
18. Do you ever remember your dreams? Do you have a particular dream that often returns? If so, how do you feel about it?
19. If you could choose just one of these, which would you choose and why? Being super handsome or attractive? Having above-average intelligence? Being famous for doing something great, or for creating something special?
20. You are allowed to change any three "things" about yourself. What would these changes be? Why?
21. How many of your friends do you believe are honest with their parents *most* of the time? If not, what sort of lies or half-truths do they tell? Tell me about your relationship with your parents *most* of the time.
22. Imagine that you had a disability. Which disability would you choose: Blind? Deaf? Inability to work? Unable to communicate clearly?
23. What is one of the most memorable moments you have experienced with a friend? Or, something a friend has unexpectedly done for you?
24. What are three qualities you believe make a great friend?
25. Imagine you are in a scary place: on a boat in stormy water; an airplane in turbulent weather; a dark area where there is no light; alone in a dark, large building—what do you think or say to yourself during such a time? (You have no cellphone.)
26. Is there any sport or other activity you have yet to try and which you believe you might be good at? Why this choice?

SECTION TWO: STRATEGIES AND TIPS TO INSPIRE

27. Do you have any pets at home? You are able to choose a special pet—not a cat, or dog, or bird. What would you choose? Why?

28. Which movies make you cry? Do you think it is okay to cry at movies? What do your friends think?

29. When you think back over the years, and the good friends you have had, who were they? Why were they good friends? What have these friendships taught you about yourself?

30. How would you describe me to your friends? (These roles can be reversed.)

31. Have you ever had a really scary dream that you can remember? What happened, or what was it all about?

32. Do you think about how intelligent you are when compared to your friends? What thoughts go through your mind?

33. Is marriage important to you? What do you think about marriage? What do you think is a good age to marry?

34. Can you remember anything about your pre-school or kindergarten experiences? Three experiences—good or not-so-good?

35. Who are the popular students in your class or year groups? Why is this? What are your thoughts about being popular?

36. You know that a friend of yours has stolen something that does not belong to them. How would you react?

37. Imagine you could be someone else for a month and live their life. Who would you choose to be, and why?

38. What is the best thing you have ever done for a family member, or a friend, or someone else? How did you feel at the time? And, now?

39. Do you have a favorite holiday you remember? Or a favorite place your family visits regularly?

40. Who do you think you are most like in your family? Your mother, father, grandparents? Why this choice?

41. Which family member makes you laugh the most? Why is this?

42. How many people are in your family, or extended family? Who do you get along best with? Why?

43. What cultural values, types of behavior, and other aspects of your culture should I be aware of?

44. How would you respond if someone falsely accused you of cheating?

45. What is the funniest experience you have ever had? Are there any life lessons you can take from that experience?

46. How important are the thoughts that your peers have about you? Why is this?

47. Are there any social influencers you follow? What are the reasons for your choice/s?

48. What issues or causes do you care about deeply, even though you may not always share this information with others?

49. Which two or three friends do you think will still be your friends twenty years from now? Why?

50. What sort of things would you either like to stop doing, or do less?

51. How do you deal with stressful situations? Can you think of a recent example?

52. What do you do or say when you become angry? What makes you angry? Shall we share ideas on how to deal with such situations?

53. When do you feel tired and listless, lacking the energy to do something? Let's consider ways to work through these times in a positive manner.

54. How many hours of sleep do you have every night? Why do you think sleep is important for brain development?

55. Have you ever experienced or heard of the term "positive stress," or "butterflies in your stomach?" Let's chat about this and share our experiences.

56. What do you most like sharing or posting with your friends online?

57. Who are the people you share your deepest thoughts with? How easy do you find this? If it is hard, how can we work out a way to make this easier in the months ahead?

58. What are you enjoying about your job? What further training do you think will help your career prospects?

59. When do you find it easiest to communicate with your parents, or caregivers, or extended family? When do you find it hardest?

SECTION TWO: STRATEGIES AND TIPS TO INSPIRE

60. How do you express your anger? What do you do or say? How do others react? How do you feel about their reactions?
61. Who deals best with conflict in your family or extended family? What can be learned from their attitude?
62. Do you have hassles or challenges with bullying at school (or in the workplace, if relevant)? How do you cope?
63. Which unresolved conflicts are you still dealing with? Shall we consider ways to work through them in the months ahead?
64. You can marry any celebrity or famous person of your choice. Who would you choose? Why?
65. Are there any friends of yours you are concerned about at the moment? Why? What can you do to support them?
66. Is there anyone at school (or at work) you would like to get to know better? Who is this person? Why would you like to know them better?
67. Would you be prepared to die for your best friend? Share the reasons for your answer.
68. How well do you get along with your siblings? When was the last time you had a strong disagreement with a sibling? What happened?
69. Are you more of an indoor or outdoor person? Why is this?
70. If you had to name one of your main weaknesses, what would you say?
71. Which is your favorite clothes shop? What was your latest purchase? How much online shopping do you do?
72. Do you have a favorite item? Jewelry? Item of clothes? Souvenir? Something you really value and would be devastated if it was broken or lost (not a cellphone)?
73. Do you receive a monthly allowance or an allowance of some sort? How do you spend it? Do you have a savings account, or ever think about learning how to budget?
74. What was the first thing that made you laugh today?
75. What do you feel is your most difficult challenge or issue you are facing at the moment?
76. Which three things can you be grateful for today?
77. What would be one of your biggest regrets to date?

TOPICS TO BUILD MEANINGFUL MENTORING RELATIONSHIPS

78. What is the most dangerous thing you have done to date?
79. You are allowed to set one family rule. What would your rule be? Why?
80. What is the best compliment you have received to date? What happened?
81. What are the qualities or characteristics you would value in someone you wish to take on a date?
82. How important do you feel cell phones are in people's lives? Do you think they help to build meaningful relationships?
83. Do you make New Year's resolutions? Have you made any this year? How are you doing?

Reflection

We seem to need mentors—wise and faithful guides, advisers or teachers—the wisdom keepers of an entire family, a sprawling corporation or a community. Much more, we need the mentor's spirit, an unseen affirming influence and positive energy. The mentor's spirit is the heart's posture pervading healthy relationships in every family, classroom, organization and town ... When the mentor's spirit is absent, we find dependency, an erosion of optimism, and impaired problem solving.

—MARSHA SINETAR[7]

iv. More general questions

1. How would you describe yourself to someone who doesn't know you?
2. How would you respond to this question (where appropriate): "If I could choose my career over again, I would choose..."
3. What is your least or most favorite form of exercise?
4. What three things need to happen for you to have a really great day?
5. What is your greatest personal achievement to date?
6. What has been the wildest prank you have ever been involved in?

7. Sinetar, *The Mentor's Spirit*.

SECTION TWO: STRATEGIES AND TIPS TO INSPIRE

7. When you were younger, what career did you want to follow when you grew up? What did your parents want you to be? And, now?
8. Where were you and what might you have been doing five years ago today?
9. You have just been offered a job at the local zoo. What animal would you like to take care of? Why?
10. If you could re-live one day of your life, which day would it be?
11. If you knew you would die tomorrow at 6.30 p.m., what would you do now?
12. Can you name one thing you wish you had been taught when you were younger?
13. Can you think about a time when a team or someone won something, and you were proud of them (you were not a member of the team)?
14. Imagine I have to introduce you to a group of people. What are the five best qualities or things about you which you would like me to share?
15. If you could tell your parents never again to serve you two specific vegetables, which would you choose and why?
16. What is your favorite meal?
17. Imagine Aladdin arrives in your home with his magic lamp. The genie appears and grants you three wishes. What would they be?
18. Have you ever been in an airplane or a helicopter? Are you scared of heights? Are you afraid to fly?
19. Have you ever been in a sailing boat, or a motor boat, or on an ocean cruise? Share your experiences.
20. Do you have your own bedroom? If you could design it any way you wished, what would you do?
21. Did you have a favorite toy when you were young? What happened to it?
22. You are in a shop and have paid for your purchase. You are given too much change. How do you respond?
23. Have you ever imitated something you have seen in a movie, TV program, X-Box or computer game? What happened?

TOPICS TO BUILD MEANINGFUL MENTORING RELATIONSHIPS

24. Many girls like to wear makeup. What do you think about this? How about boys wearing makeup?
25. Can you think of a really embarrassing moment in your life? What happened?
26. What age do you think should be allowed for a person to watch any movie of their choice? What do your friends do? How would your parents respond to this question?
27. You have just won the $1 million lottery prize. What would you do with the money?
28. Who is your favorite cartoon character?
29. A friend gives you $1 million to give to a charity or charities of your choice. How would you allocate the money?
30. Do you have any household chores or duties to carry out? What are they?
31. Are you familiar with the term "bucket list"—things you would like to do in your lifetime? What would be the top six items on your bucket list if you wrote one today?
32. Do you have a favorite restaurant? Why this choice?
33. What would be the weirdest or strangest meal you have ever had?
34. Would you rather live in the mountains, or by the sea, or in a city, or town, or in the countryside? Why this choice?
35. Can you think of times when you wished you were either a few years older or younger? What caused these thoughts?
36. Would you rather be the owner (the boss) or the employee? Why?
37. Which college or university would you like to attend? Why? Shall we look at their website and find out more information? (A mentor shares why and how they chose the college or university they attended—where relevant.)
38. You have one opportunity to give one gift to everyone in the world. The gift can be anything at all. What would you choose?
39. Think back to three years ago. What advice would you give yourself?
40. You have the power to introduce just one rule that the global community must follow. What would be that one rule?

41. Would you ever get a tattoo? Why, or why not? What would it be? Where would you place it?
42. How do you respond to the statement: "Students should be allowed to grade their teachers?"
43. Let's look at this world map and share our hopes, dreams, and travel experiences. (A mentor encourages their mentee to think of future possibilities and opportunities.)

Reflection

John Maxwell [leadership expert and author] says the average person impacts more than 10,000 people in their lifetime. That's significant! Therefore, change your world. This is a major step in changing the world of others, many of whom you will never know, by the words you use and the deeds you do.

—[ADAPTED] ZIG ZIGLAR

v. Questions: deeper topics

Adolescents experience many times of confusion as their brains develop. They try to understand themselves, and wonder how they will fit into an adult world of work, and responsibility. This is a daunting prospect for many young people.

Mentors can play a significant role in this journey. Mentors consistently model their values—never enforcing them on their mentees—share their knowledge and skills, talk about their work and adult experiences, and the behavior expected in the wider community, and support young people to take charge of their choices. Paul Browning offers some sage advice: "No one enjoys being micro-managed. Your job as a leader [mentor] is not to create a "mini-me" but to empower others, enabling them to flourish and contribute their own unique dispositions, gifts and capabilities to their work."[8]

This time of authentic sharing is a significant help to the mentee's personal development.

---

8. Browning, *Principled*, 57.

This modeling can also make a significant impact on the lives of mentees from low socio-economic, or high-risk environments who experience little contact with positive adult role models. Author Pat O'Brien comments that "Kids don't need independence, they need interdependence. ... Who in this society can live independently? All human beings want to belong somewhere."

The questions that follow create a deeper sense of connectedness between a mentor and a young person.

Mentors learn how to authentically paint a positive picture of their mentees' lives one day in the global community—a powerful envisioning process—and, where possible, take them out of their communities to visit other communities where their mentees might aspire to live at some stage in the future.

Some of the key signs of a positive self-image a mentor can watch developing in their mentee during a meaningful relationship can include the mentee:

- taking acceptable risks that are not life-threatening;
- risking a move out of their comfort zone;
- handling mistakes in a positive and constructive manner;
- sticking at tasks and goals until they have finished or achieved them;
- standing up to negative peer pressure.

1. When you look up at the sky, what do you think is beyond the stars? Would you ever like to visit the moon? Why? How do you think the universe was created?
2. How do you respond to the statement: "Global climate change is man-made"?
3. What do you think are the arguments for and against Artificial Intelligence (AI)?
4. How do you respond to the statement: "Professional athletes, actors, and celebrities are paid too much"?
5. At what age should parents allow their teenage children to make their own decisions?
6. There are a variety of opinions about the legal age for drinking alcohol. What are your thoughts?

SECTION TWO: STRATEGIES AND TIPS TO INSPIRE

7. Do you attend a single gender or co-educational school? What do you think are the positives and possible negatives of these school systems?
8. What do you think are the arguments for and against students having to wear a school uniform?
9. How important do you think competition is in a child's education? Do you have any personal experiences to share?
10. There is an opinion that students should not have to do homework. What are your thoughts?
11. How do you respond to the statement: "Animals should never be used for research"?
12. Do you believe we have a "throw-away" society? How do you think this issue can be better addressed—imagine you are a government minister responsible for environmental matters?
13. Should all governments provide free schooling, and university (or post-school training), as well as free health care? If so, how should this be funded?
14. Let's talk about our country's election process. What do you know about it? What age do you think should be the minimum voting age?
15. Do you think a lottery is a good idea? What are the arguments in favor of or against a lottery? Would you buy a ticket for a national lottery each week, maybe even twice a week if you were allowed to do so?
16. There is a suggestion that violent video games make people more violent. What are your thoughts? What video games do you enjoy, and how do they affect you?
17. How do you think photoshopped images might impact our thinking about ourselves? How do these images affect you?
18. If you were given a choice between home schooling or a school education, what would you choose? Why?
19. What do you know and think about ChatGPT (or other technological programs young people are accessing at the time)? Positives? Negatives? Things to be aware of?
20. How effective do you think the death penalty is? What do you think about the death penalty where countries have this?
21. When do you think torture might be justifiable?

22. What are your opinions about vaping and cigarette smoking? Should they be banned?

Reflection

Fundamentally, a mentor connects a mentee to resources: his or her own personal network .... libraries, helpful videos, audio tapes [YouTube clips] and books, even support groups. The mentor is never required to have all the answers or all the resources. They are simply a connector to many resources that the mentee needs during the growth process. As a mentor, your attitude should be: "I'm here to help you, and I'll do what I can."

—Bobb Biehl[9]

---

9. Biehl, *Mentoring*.

3. Responsible use of social media

As a species we are very highly attuned to reading social cues. There is no question kids are missing out on very critical social skills. In a way, texting and online communicating—it's not like it creates a nonverbal learning disability, but it puts everybody in a nonverbal disabled context, where body language, facial expression, and even the smallest kinds of vocal reactions are rendered invisible.

—CATHERINE STEINER-ADAIR, CLINICAL PSYCHOLOGIST[1]

How many teenagers do you know who have ended up in trouble because their online behavior has been inappropriate? I recall a situation where fifteen-year-old Alice videoed an unpleasant altercation between two students, shared it on a social media platform and, within a few minutes, it was being shared and distributed by her peers. When a colleague and I shared what had happened with Alice's mother, the latter was in denial and blamed us for the way we had handled the matter. How did we handle the matter? Alice had admitted her poor judgment. My colleague and I arranged with another colleague who had extensive knowledge and experience in the responsible use of social media to meet with Alice and share some thoughts.

Fourteen-year-old Maeve lent her phone to Liam who discovered an inappropriate photograph of Maeve and forwarded it on to a friend of his, who then passed it around. It had a sad ending, as the school expelled the students involved, not a decision I would support in most cases, as schools and families should see themselves as people tasked with educating young

1. Ehmke, *How Using Social Media.*

people on how to use technology responsibly. Two young lives—and the lives of their families—were severely impacted by a moment of indecision or thoughtlessness, a lifelong lesson hopefully learnt as well: *every choice has a consequence.*

Something I have learned over the years is that many young people are not as technologically savvy as we think they are, though, in reality, all of us need to be better digital citizens. A number of young people are fairly ignorant of some basic common-sense behaviors one should follow when using technology, despite the fact that they are regarded as "digital natives" who have, from an early age, grown up with the internet, smartphones, social media platforms, and a variety of apps and other online communication tools.

Promoting anxiety and lowering self-esteem

It is common knowledge that the inappropriate use of social media can promote anxiety and lower self-esteem in teenage lives. It can also lead to unnecessary distractions—from academic studies, for example—disrupt sleep patterns, and expose youth, according to Mayo Clinic staff in the USA, to "bullying, rumor spreading, unrealistic views of other people's lives and [negative] peer pressure." A report by the Mayo Clinic states:

> A 2019 study of more than 6,500 12-to 15-year-olds in the U.S. found that those who spent more than three hours a day using social media might be at heightened risk for mental health problems. Another 2019 study of more than 12,000 13- to 16-year-olds in England found that using social media more than three times a day predicted poor mental health and well-being in teens.[2]

Another article about how social media affects teenagers noted:

> A survey by the Royal Society for Public Health asked 14-24-year-olds in the UK how social media platforms impacted their health and wellbeing. The survey results found that Snapchat, Facebook, Twitter and Instagram all led to increased feelings of depression, anxiety, poor body image, and loneliness.[3]

The teenage brain is at a key point of development, and the prefrontal cortex, where planning and decision-making occurs, is maturing until the

2. Mayo Clinic, *Tween and Teen Health.*
3. Ehmke, *How Using Social Media.*

mid-twenties. Therefore, teenagers tend to react more emotionally to issues going on in their lives than adults would, which partly explains the hurtful and emotional outbursts on social media. Clinical and developmental psychologist Donna Wick explains: "Kids text all sorts of things that you would never in a million years contemplate saying to anyone's face [especially true of girls]."[4]

Some reasons teenagers use social media

Do you have enough digital literacy to know when you are being manipulated or not?

There are many reasons why teenagers—indeed, most of us—use social media, though the most common reasons include:

- having fun;
- connecting with friends and sharing their creativity;
- joining group chats, or gaming chat sites, and meeting new people;
- peer pressure—creating a belief that those who are not on social media will miss out in some way or other;
- wanting to find out information about current events;
- undertaking some research for an assignment, or in an area of interest— supported by an important strategy and tip offered by educators Magdalena Brzezinska and Edward Cremarty from their research: "Offering equal access to technology and learning opportunities is a crucial ingredient in nurturing a sensitive environment in which all students are welcome to become active participants."[5]
- linking to a support network;
- feeling bored and having nothing to do;
- sharing hobbies, music, and other interests.

---

4. Ehmke, *How Using Social Media*.
5. Brzezinska and Cromarty, *Emergency Remote Teaching*, 44.

Positive benefits from the responsible use of social media

There are many positive benefits of the responsible and safe use of social media we can share with young people. Some of these benefits include:

- being better equipped to become active, responsible, and respectful global citizens in a global community driven by technology;
- the development of innovative and creativity skills which are critically important for future careers. These skills can include being creative with profile pages, images, videos, modifying games—perhaps even creating a new game;
- learning: understanding digital media literacy in a safe and secure environment. This can include developing social media skills, learning how to gain enjoyment from the positive use of social media online activities, and gaining a deeper understanding of online risks and how to respond to them;
- positive connections with extended family, friends, a mentor, or within safe local and global online communities. These connections create a sense of belonging and can have a positive impact on a teenager's health and wellbeing;
- the development of real-world skills to encourage them to become more resilient and independent.

There is enough research to show how social media plays a significant role in the creative and social lives of young people. A mentor—or teacher, parent, youth worker, or coach—can have repeated conversations about the responsible use of social media with their mentee and, as they build a relationship of trust, the mentee might ask more questions, reveal concerns, or share some challenging experiences as they try and understand the enormous responsibility every individual should feel when communicating respectfully and safely with others via social media. These conversations are more important in the post-pandemic global community, as young people have experienced a variety of reactions to lockdowns, and being isolated from face-to-face relationships with their peers.

SECTION TWO: STRATEGIES AND TIPS TO INSPIRE

Discussion suggestions about the responsible use of social media

Here are some opinions about the responsible and respectful use of technology, which anyone working with young people can discuss with them. While it would be best for a parent to discuss these with their children, this is not always possible. The discussion can take a variety of forms and be repeated. Mentors, who communicate online with their mentees, can model effective communication techniques and skills, and chat regularly about how their mentee can monitor their own online presence.

1. Make sure all your privacy settings are activated on all social media sites you use, so that people you don't know will be unable to see your posts. Keep checking your profile and remove anything that might be too personal or inappropriate.
2. Never give out any of your log-in details or passwords to friends, or anyone you meet online.
3. Use different usernames and passwords to protect yourself from hackers. If you think your profile is being hacked, change passwords immediately.
4. Don't use silly email addresses, especially if you are applying for scholarships, awards, or jobs.
5. Only accept friend requests from real friends you personally know. Even then, check their profile before accepting.
6. Never give away your phone number or home address online.
7. Only download software after you have discussed this with your parents, or an adult you trust.
8. Remember that everything you post online is *public*. It makes no difference whether or not you delete it at some time in the future. It can be traced back to you.
9. Be highly selective of what you post online. Is it age appropriate? Will your parents approve? Never post anything online or send anything you would be embarrassed for anyone important to you to see. When in doubt, check with your parents or an adult you trust. A good rule is never to post images of others without their permission.
10. Avoid going into chat rooms and revealing personal information about yourself. Many people who go online lie about who they really are.

RESPONSIBLE USE OF SOCIAL MEDIA

11. Never post anything online when you are angry, so you don't say anything you might regret later. Also, don't respond to anything online when you are emotionally charged up in any way.

12. Avoid responding to messages online that are unkind, hurtful, or potentially damaging either to you or others. If you are concerned about a message, talk to your parents or an adult you trust. Stay true to the Golden Rule: "Do to others what you would like them to do to you." *Pause before you post!*

13. Avoid speaking about your personal problems or challenges with your friends online. Rather phone or chat face-to-face—it's safer.

14. Avoid speaking to strangers online—and never agree to meet someone that you have met online if you don't know them in real life. Speak to your parents or an adult you trust immediately if one of these people wants to meet up with you.

15. Avoid posting or sending inappropriate images, videos—even messages—as you might be breaking the law and end up in trouble with the police, especially if you are underage. Discuss the responsible use of emojis, GIFs (animated images), and memes with your mentor or a responsible adult. If you receive inappropriate posts, tell your parents or an adult you trust immediately, or take screenshots to discuss with people you trust. Also, disable features such as posting to multiple social media sites immediately.

16. Don't overshare on social media. People don't really want to know everything you are doing for every minute of the day. Social media is not only about you.

17. Negotiate the use of a computer and cellphone at home with your parents, as this will build trust and responsibility, and assist your adolescent journey to independence or interdependence.

18. Remember to logout when you use public computers, such as in a public library or a place of study.

19. Avoid clicking on pop-ups, as some of these may appear friendly and safe, though can lead to requests for more personal information, or link you to pornography sites.

20. Place your cellphone and computer in another room at night, as you need nine hours sleep *every* night, so your brain can be cleaned out ready for the new day.

These points can lead to further interesting discussions about the use of technology, and how one develops a responsible and safe digital footprint.

Mentors and mentees can negotiate how they will communicate online when in a face-to-face relationship. Mentees are likely to respond and welcome "short" texts, though the timing and sending of these texts is something that needs to be agreed on by both parties. A mentee, for example, might be disappointed if their mentor does not respond to a text message relatively quickly, and this could have a negative impact on their relationship. Michelle Kaufman offers some helpful advice to mentors: "Allowing a mentee to see your online presence is a great opportunity to model how to be engaged online in a safe, appropriate way."[6]

A further point to encourage young people to develop their potential linked to the choices they make "offline," has been suggested by writer Rachel Ehmke[7]:

> … the gold standard advice for helping kids build healthy self-esteem is to get them involved in something that they're interested in. It could be sports or music or taking apart computers or volunteering—anything that sparks an interest and gives them confidence. When kids learn to feel good about what they can do instead of how they look and what they own, they're happier and better prepared for success in real life. That most of these activities also involve spending time interacting with peers face-to-face is just the icing on the cake.

Reflection

Mentors also help us see ourselves in ways we can't on our own. At any age, we can find a mentor in life. If we don't have access to a mentor in person, we can experience the wisdom of a mentor through the written word.

—Tina Turner[8]

---

6. Kaufman, *Becoming a Better Mentor.*
7. Ehmke, *How Using Social Media.*
8. Turner, *Happiness Becomes You,* 102.

4. How to achieve greatness—winning ways to share with young people

How often in your life have you come close to achieving a goal and either slipped up at the last moment, or felt it was too hard to achieve and given up?

There have been times in my life when I have failed to achieve my potential through moments of self-doubt, or not pushing myself that "little" bit harder. Then I have experienced the "what if?" moments. What if I had not walked up that hill during a cross-country race? What if I had stood up and expressed my honest opinion about that matter?

Thomas Edison founder of General Electric famously once stated: "Many of life's failures are men who didn't realize how close they were to success when they gave up."

There are many stories about people who have overcome tough times and achieved much with their lives. I love these stories, and young people will also enjoy hearing them. They are inspirational and motivating, and a continual reminder that each one of us is unique, has gifts and talents and, when we choose to chase our dreams, we can achieve a great deal.

Not too long ago I watched golfer Richard Bland, aged forty-eight at the time, playing his 478th tournament on the European Tour, having never won. He emerged as the oldest first-time winner on the European Tour, a wonderful example of perseverance and persistence over more than twenty years as a golfer chasing a dream to win a tournament on the European Tour. He has bounced back from a number of setbacks over the years, so there was little surprise when he shed a few tears after winning the tournament at the first play-off hole. A great story to share with young people, many of whom do not yet understand how hard they must practice, or study to achieve their goals. Behind many great achievers' stories will be times of self-sacrifice, failure, even self-doubt.

SECTION TWO: STRATEGIES AND TIPS TO INSPIRE

Life is about striving to reach our unique potential—an individual's "greatness." It's not about being successful, when success is measured by how much money we have, or what car we drive, or the size of our house. It is more about becoming the best person we can possibly be, or, to express this another way, *simple* greatness is the best greatness. And this is why mentors are important as the "wise guides on the side" of young people trying to find their way, all the more so during these challenging times when more and more young people (especially young adults), would welcome a non-judgmental, empathetic person to help and encourage them to chase their dream.

A good friend and former teaching colleague Gordon Paterson spent time reflecting on a season in his life as a teacher and sports coach. His reflection serves as a wonderful guide to mentors, a check-list too during the mentoring journey:

> I am fulfilled and I am blessed if I have imparted to any of the young people I have coached and taught the assurance that:
>
> - in times of necessity there is a great source of strength to be drawn from;
> - in times of triumph there is a need to be humble and thankful;
> - the road to follow includes the strength of peace and the good of love;
> - enjoyment comes from accepting the challenge to be the best we can;
> - while we must contribute fully towards our destiny, we are not in complete control;
> - winners in life will often be beaten in the sport arena, and they win in life by attending to their own performance and assisting others to victory, rather than focusing their energies on superiority over others;
> - they belong and are lovable, capable, and unique in the special talents they offer.[1]

Encourage young people to discover their passion, chase their dreams and then watch as doors open, opportunities come their way, and they enjoy their career journey. They are emboldened to remember the importance of relationships in their lives when they do this, valuing the non-judgmental voice of a cheerleader when they experience the inevitable setbacks, stumbles, and challenging times.

---

1. Paterson, *There is Genius*, 338-339.

Mentors can remind mentees to nurture the people that really matter to them. Communicate with them. Ask them to share their life stories. Bounce ideas off them and listen, listen, listen.

I read plenty of stories about achievers. Some I truly admire, others I do not admire at all. I have no respect for those who make their fortune by exploiting others, cheating, doing illegal stuff, or treating employees badly. I can share my thoughts with mentees—and they will soon understand my values—though must never force my opinions on them.

Image, image, image! How many people are more worried about their image than about being true to themselves? This is often evident in the world of pop stars, celebrities and the so-called glamorous "Hollywood life" which is promoted even more by social media platforms, and media personalities.

Here are some key thoughts mentors can use as they encourage mentees to take responsibility, and become accountable for their choices on their journey to achieve simple greatness, or reach their unique potential. It is also a useful checklist which mentees can discuss and share with their friends. Each of these points can create great discussion points during the mentoring journey.

Winning ways to achieve simple greatness

1. I am working at becoming a genuinely positive person with a positive self-image.
2. I am living for today and taking responsibility for my life.
3. I am a dreamer imagining where I will be in one month, three months, five years from now.
4. I have set my specific, measurable, realistic, achievable goals and have a timetable for achieving them.
5. I am enjoying life to the full, making good friends, and reaching out to others in need of help.
6. I am working at my self-discipline.
7. I believe in myself more and more each day.
8. I know my strengths and the areas I need to improve.

9. I am unafraid to make decisions, think things out for myself, while appreciating feedback in areas I could improve.
10. I am flexible, and a good team player.
11. My behavior is consistent and predictable *most* of the time.
12. I am developing the qualities of trustworthiness, honesty, humility, empathy, and self-reliance.
13. I know myself, back myself, and believe in myself—I am capable and lovable.
14. I enjoy my work, and am comfortable and self-confident in the company of others.
15. I am prepared to take calculated and non-life-threatening risks.
16. I dare to be different.
17. I am prepared to move out of my comfort zone.
18. I follow a healthy and balanced lifestyle.[2]

Reflection

Mentors can provide a safe haven for teens to air sensitive issues (about self and in their understanding of others—for example, parents, teachers, siblings and peers) while still transmitting adult values, advice and perspectives ... By providing their point of view in a supportive, trusting context, mentors can help adolescents successfully balance autonomy with closeness in their interactions with their parents. And unlike parental advice, which adolescents are often quick to dismiss, guidance and encouragement from a non-parent adult is sometimes taken more to heart.

—JEAN E. RHODES[3]

---

2. Cox, *Letter 2 a Teen*, 52.
3. Rhodes, *Stand by Me*.

SECTION THREE
Mentoring in action

This section offers a variety of stories to show mentoring in action, and reminds anyone working with young people that every young person is unique, and brings a personal story to their relationship. True mentoring stories and analogies are packed with strategies and tips to build positive relationships with young people, supporting and encouraging them to reach their potential. Most people love hearing true stories. Some of these stories can be woven into discussions with the young people we care about. There are best practices one can strive to achieve when moving alongside a young person in a formal or informal mentoring role, even as a parent who is expected to offer their child unconditional love. Anxiety has been identified as one of the key issues young people have to deal with, made worse in many cases by the recent pandemic, lockdowns, wars, environmental disasters, and refugee crises. A few strategies and tips on how to approach stress and anxiety, examples of people who have overcome potential stressful situations and adversity to achieve greatness, and many supportive thoughts for anyone undertaking a mentoring role, complete this section.

You must take personal responsibility. You cannot change the circumstances, the seasons or the wind, but you can change yourself. That is something you have charge of. You don't have charge of the constellations, but you do have charge of whether you read, develop new skills, and take new classes.
—JIM ROHN

1. Listening to that inner voice— a true story

Throughout your life, there is a voice you can hear. A voice which mythologists label "the call." A call to the value of your life. The choice of risk and individual bliss over the known and secure. You may choose not to hear your spirit. You may prefer to build a life within the compound, to avoid risk. It is possible to find happiness within a familiar box, a life of comfort and control. Or you may choose to be open to new experiences, to leave the limits of your conditioning, to hear the call. Then you must act. If you never hear it, perhaps nothing is lost. If you hear it and ignore it, your life is lost.

—JENNIFER JAMES[1]

Do you ever have those moments when your inner voice is urging you to do something, and you fail to act? Over the years I have learnt how to listen to my inner voice and act, even if there might be some risk involved.

My day begins with a quiet, reflective time, and then I head out for a walk by the sea. Often the rising sun produces some spectacular sunrises, reminding me how privileged I am to live where I do.

One morning the inner voice was speaking and, when I went for my walk, it seemed to persist, so I decided to obey. Lucy was turning seventeen later that year, in her final year of school, and had been doing it tough for quite some time, mostly dealing with difficult family relationships. Yet, despite these struggles, she produced better than average academic results, evidence of a resilient spirit.

1. James, *Living Life Fully*.

SECTION THREE: MENTORING IN ACTION

One relationship that is important to most young women approaching adulthood is the relationship with their mother. I sensed Lucy's relationship with her mother was fragmented. As a result, Lucy was riding an emotional rollercoaster which resulted in antisocial behavior tendencies, significant mood swings, and always the possibility of inappropriate behavior.

I had not had much to do with Lucy. I had never taught her, and had only spoken to her when she was included in a discussion I had with another student.

I had watched her represent a school sports team, and observed her enthusiasm and her enjoyment participating as a member of that team. I had watched her earlier that week swimming in the school's annual carnival in which most students participate no matter how good or weak they are at swimming. Lucy swam impressively, definitely doing her best in the events in which she participated.

I had heard a fairly reliable rumor—shared by a student in her friendship group—that Lucy and her mother had had another fall out. Assuming that Lucy's mother was wobbling on the day, she had evidently said that she wished Lucy had never been born, a comment that Lucy had overheard and, quite naturally, had left an already vulnerable girl feeling more fragile, and having a bit of a melt-down at school the next day.

When the inner voice told me to email—via the school's safe and secure email system—a word of encouragement to Lucy that morning, I decided to do so.

An edited version of what I shared with Lucy went something like this:

> I have watched you participating in some of your school matches and then at the swimming carnival, and I just wanted to congratulate you on the way you give everything your best shot. It is great to see and it also looks as though you are enjoying the participation too.
>
> Clearly you have plenty of talent, and I hope that you will continue to develop it during the remaining months of your final year at school.
>
> When you walk out of the final Assembly at the end of the year, I hope you will do so with no regrets, knowing you have seized every opportunity available to you, and made the most of the year, including gaining the academic results you are striving to achieve.
>
> I always encourage students, in their final year of school, to surround themselves with positive peers who are striving to become the best they can be. That leads to positive mindsets, and

positive relationships which carry them through the challenging times.

The younger students are probably looking up at you with respect and admiration, and I hope you might inspire some of them to step up and give everything their best shot as well.

Well done on all you are achieving!

I added two posters with the following anonymous quotes:

"Believe in yourself and all that you are. Know that there is something inside you that is greater than any obstacle."

and

"Rise up and be the best you can because your world is waiting for you."

I have no idea how Lucy reacted to this email and the attachments. I might never know, as I retired soon after sending it, another reason why I obeyed my inner voice.

My hope is that she printed out the content, kept it in a safe place, and read it again and again when she felt disheartened, unloved, vulnerable, or battered like the rocks in the raging tide. I also hope she received it as a message of encouragement to continue developing the tremendous talent she has, and that it was a reminder to *never* quit.

Why share this?

The spirit of mentoring has taught me the power of being an encourager and cheerleader and, when it might be a risk sending a positive message of *hope* and encouragement, that's a calculated risk worth taking, as it might even be life-changing.

How about you? When last did you obey the inner voice? What happened?

Reflection

Resilience is not something that can be taught; the better way is to grow resilience by ensuring the school as an organization nurtures individual and group connectivity and support. The mixed-age base provides the security needed for such a task and a secure base to venture out and return.

—PETER BARNARD[2]

2. Barnard, *Socially Collaborative Schools*, 53.

2. Becoming resilient—Barry's story

There are many challenges facing adolescents between the ages of eleven and nineteen. This highlights the important role a mentor plays in that young life. Here are some challenges most young people confront, which I have gathered from years of research, confirmed by my own mentoring, coaching, and teaching experiences.

- A child deprived of unconditional love in the development years is often unable to relate effectively to others, or to love themselves.
- A child who has not received love, frequently finds it difficult to give love.
- Children who do not feel valued often do not value themselves or others.
- The adolescent years involve testing new beliefs, new systems, and new ways of operating and behaving, and finding out what other ways of life are like. It is better to experiment with, and learn life lessons from these experiences within the safety and security of family, or extended family structures.
- Children must have opportunities to face the consequences of their behavior if they are to become responsible young people. Policy analyst and author, Jennifer Buckingham stated:

    > The child with a strong, affectionate family, whose parents care for his or her welfare, and supervise his or her behavior and schooling, is more likely to be successful at school, less likely to become suicidal, and less likely to fall into delinquency and juvenile crime. Such a family is a protective and positive factor in every sense. …
    >
    > For boys particularly, the absence of a father in the home is a deprivation. Whether we like it or not, it still makes sense to speak

of a masculine culture and of ideals of manhood to which most boys aspire, be it consciously or unconsciously. Boys look for models and guidance from the men and other boys with whom they have contact. But if such contact is devoid of strength of character, or if it is emotionally and morally "thin", a developmental influence of the greatest importance will be missing or misdirected.[1]

How well I remember Barry, aged fifteen, and a real handful. Barry's attitude and behavior frustrated and annoyed his teachers to the point that they no longer wanted him in the classroom. As I was the school principal, Barry became my challenge. Ought I to keep him in the school, or ask his parents to remove him? How much more disruption could we tolerate, especially as Barry's behavior was negatively impacting the learning opportunities of his peers in his classes?

Firstly, I had to speak to Barry.

I recall how we sat chatting in my office for about two hours. Our discussion covered a variety of topics, though I kept bringing the conversation back to the fact that, if Barry chose to remain at the school, he needed to understand the importance of becoming a positive member of the community. My role was to encourage Barry to appreciate how discipline—and self-discipline—is the doorway to freedom.

I often ask this question when I talk about discipline issues with uncooperative students: *imagine what would happen if cars arrived at a four-way intersection, all the traffic lights were broken and the drivers decided to keep on driving. What would the result be?*

Of course, the answer is that there would be road carnage. I explain to the student that, in the same way as the roads have rules, so do schools. It's in the best interests of the community if students cooperate and support the rules that were, in fact, agreed on by the majority of students at the beginning of each school year.

In this particular school at the beginning of each year students were divided into groups of between ten and fifteen, and they would spend a few hours with a tutor discussing the school's Code of Conduct. I would collate the results of the discussions, and then the Parent, Teacher, Student Committee would give their input before the Code of Conduct was finalized and distributed to all parents, students, and teachers.

Barry understood all this and we parted on positive terms, though I did tell him that I would have to meet with his parents to discuss his

---

1. Buckingham, *Boy Troubles*.

behavior. If his negative, insolent behavior continued—an attitude choice he was making—I would suspend him from school, and his parents had to understand this.

These difficult conversations with young people—more of an informal spirit of mentoring moment—have the potential to become life-changing moments. Barry and I had had a lengthy conversation covering many topics. Perhaps Barry felt respected, that his ideas and opinions mattered, and appreciated that his teachers and other authority figures genuinely cared for him. Perhaps Barry began to realize that he had the ability to see solutions as well as obstacles, and to be more proactive with his choices. He certainly knew that his future choices would have consequences.

It took a few days to contact Barry's parents and arrange a chat. They were polite, supportive, and understanding.

Only after I had met the parents did I hear that Barry's father had an alcohol problem and, whenever he started drinking, Barry would flee the house in terror, sometimes not even sleeping at home on a particular evening. Yet he would be at school the next day. Had I known that, I would have called Barry in again and told him how I admired his courage and perseverance in coming to school on time in such difficult circumstances. Certainly, Barry's home difficulties explained some of his antisocial behavior.

Barry's behavior improved and, when I left the school some months later, and went to fetch my daughter from a party one evening, there was Barry. He approached my car, put his hand through the open window and shook my hand warmly. He thanked me for all I had done for him, and genuinely wished me happiness in the future.

I often think about Barry and wonder what he is doing these days, as he is now a middle-aged man.

Barry's story is about resiliency, having the ability to bounce back from tough times, and to appreciate that every choice he made had a consequence. If I knew then what I know now about resiliency, I could have contributed a significant amount to Barry's life by identifying at least one of his resilient qualities—one of his strengths. He would then have learned how, when the going was tough, that *one* special resilient quality could help him bounce back.

Hopefully, through our interactions, Barry picked up some of the seeds of the spirit of mentoring which he could pass on to his generation.

Reflection

Teens are hungry for role models outside their own families. They are developing an increased capacity for empathy, intimacy and problem-solving, all of which contribute to resilience. They are testing their own sense of competence as never before. With the right guidance, they can learn to draw on the inner qualities and outer resources that constitute resilience.

—(ARTICLE) COMPETENT KIDS[2]

---

2. Institute for Mental Health Initiatives, *Competent Kids*.

3. Handling peer pressure—Rachel's, Chris's, and Linda's stories

For most of my teaching career I worked in high or secondary schools attended by students between the ages of twelve and nineteen. One of the greatest issues I confronted was the effect of peer pressure on the lives of these young people.

It's seen in the negative attitude to almost anything that is said. It's seen in the way students who want to ask questions, or become involved in an activity, or respond to a question, remain silent for fear of being mocked, or taunted by their peers. It's supposedly not "cool" to try too hard.

I heard the story about Rachel who excelled at primary school. However, when she moved to high school she scraped through her exams—50 percent, 51 percent, or similar results. When challenged, she admitted that she did not want to lose her friends, so she was just doing enough to get through.

And what happened to Rachel? During her penultimate year at school, she realized she was not fulfilling her potential, stepped aside from the negative peer pressure, and surrounded herself with positive peers. She became a positive and influential leader in her final year at school, achieved excellent academic results, and continued this excellence at university and into the workplace.

The mentor's challenge is to encourage their mentee to reach their potential, and this involves some significant personal choices. Graham Coyle shared how an influential teacher impacted his young life: "I did catch something from him and it was this, the desire to see other people achieve more than they ever thought was possible."[1]

---

1. Coyle, *To Infinity*.

What I have seen over the years in young people who make those significant personal choices has been quite amazing.

Chris joined a mentoring program I was running. He had started abusing alcohol, getting into trouble with his parents and school authorities, and being negatively impacted by peer pressure.

During the nine months Chris was part of the mentoring program, his volunteer adult mentor, Ray, spent time exploring Chris' interests, looking at what was possible, trying to identify and name his strengths, and a whole lot more. Ray helped Chris work through all the issues that were leading to his antisocial behavior.

At all times Chris made the final choices about his behavior. On occasions his choices might not have been the best. However, when the mentoring program formally ended, Chris acknowledged that he was focused on going to university to obtain an Engineering degree.

Chris also shared how Ray had helped him realize that he was wasting his talents and potential hanging out with disruptive and negative *so-called* friends, most of whom were going nowhere fast, were likely to make some costly mistakes, and probably would not reach their potential.

Chris, encouraged by a non-judgmental cheerleader, made some crucial choices at just the right time in his life.

> Young people need someone to sit down with them and point out the options and the opportunities. They have to learn to be flexible and open to change and to be prepared. A mentor helps you to find and define your center, to set goals, and to articulate what you want to be in life.
> —Thomas Minter

Linda was in a similar situation, though she was lying and vandalizing property so she could stay "cool" with her friends.

Linda embarked on a similar journey to that experienced by Chris with her mentor, Patti.

Patti asked some tough questions and refused to listen to any lying or excuses Linda might offer. Patti spoke to the potential Linda was unable to see at that time.

Patti helped Linda gain some work experience at a hairdressing salon, as Linda was interested in that type of work. By the end of the mentoring program, Linda was a happy, more motivated young woman on the road to reaching her potential. She had responded positively to Patti's non-judgmental and caring attitude. Linda was eventually offered a casual position at the hairdressing salon because of her newly developed positive attitude.

    Both Linda and Chris also learned how to become goal getters, which significantly affected their attitude to school, family, and to life in general.

Reflection

One mentee described how shocked and happy he was to receive a phone call from his ultra-busy mentor. "I couldn't believe it. He called me from the airport just to say he was thinking about me and ask how my game went. I think that was one of the best parts of our relationship. He made me feel like what was going on in my life was really important to him."

    —LINDA PHILLIPS-JONES[2]

---

2. Phillips-Jones, *100 Ideas*, 3.

4. Becoming a positive role model—Jason's story

Jason, a young boy in a mentoring program with which I was involved, chose a policeman as his mentor. When questioned about his choice, he said that he knew he needed discipline in his life. He was making poor choices and he believed the policeman would help him make the right choices for his future.

Jason shared that he was failing all his subjects when he joined the mentoring program, and was also hanging around with members of a gang. As he and his mentor, Gavin, developed the mentoring relationship, Jason began to appreciate that he was talented, bright, and was underachieving badly at school. He was also negatively influenced by his peers.

Jason had to make some tough choices. Six months later he achieved distinctions in most of his academic subjects and had changed his peer group. He was thinking seriously, even exploring the possibility of one day studying medicine.

Gavin had played a key role as a non-judgmental cheerleader in Jason's life, helping him to develop more self-discipline, manage his time more effectively, set achievable goals, and reconsider his friendships—many choices. Gavin had observed Jason maturing into a more assertive young man with the ability to stand up for himself, his beliefs, his ideas and opinions (even when under stress) without violating the rights of others in any way. He observed how Jason was acquiring the ability to cope with life's challenges as his self-confidence improved, and he developed a more positive self-image—indicators of the power of mentoring.

Jason's only regret was that his negative peers would not listen to him when he tried to encourage them to change their ways.

SECTION THREE: MENTORING IN ACTION

Reflection

I tell you I think we all learned so much from this whole experience. With kids, you have to be so mindful, whether you are raising them, mentoring them, caring for them or teaching them. You've got to check that ego at the door and listen, listen very carefully.

—Unknown mentor

5. From teenage rebel to achiever—Jess's story

I sometimes reflect on the stories of students I have worked with in years gone by and wonder where they are today. This tends to happen when I receive an email out of the blue from a student who left school a while ago, and wants to connect about a personal matter they are dealing with, as happened with Jess.

Fifteen-year-old Jess was above average academically, usually did well in exams, but was unmotivated. She was a talented musician with great potential.

However, her parents had divorced and she began to rebel against her mother's discipline. Indeed, she became something of a rebellious spirit at school.

She initially rejected some goal-setting ideas. However, when really on the slide, she decided to seek some assistance, looked at her strengths and weaknesses, and set some challenging goals for herself.

Jess went from strength to strength, gained academic distinctions in four of her six subjects, was appointed to a position of leadership in the school, joined the school choir, and became secretary to a number of school clubs or societies.

Furthermore, Jess worked hard at improving her communication with her mother.

Life lessons from Jess's experience

Looking back, what can be concluded from Jess's experience to support those who move alongside challenging young people for a season of their youth?

SECTION THREE: MENTORING IN ACTION

- Jess was a normal teenager journeying through the confusing adolescent years as her brain developed. She was gifted in a number of areas and was probably fortunate in that she could cope with her academic studies.
- Jess, though, was unhappy within. Perhaps she saw some of her friends enjoying positive family relationships, something she did not experience as her parents were divorced. Sometimes this can lead to a period of confusion, anger, frustration, and antisocial behavior tendencies.
- Jess was like most teenagers. She believed she was okay, had the answers, and no adults could ever understand how she was feeling.
- Jess came close to hitting rock bottom. Her rebellious attitude, which she had chosen, was getting her nowhere other than in continuous trouble. Thankfully, she reached a point when she realized that she needed some assistance. Once she found that assistance, she discovered that she was not being judged, and that there was someone listening respectfully to her, guiding her, and willing to journey with her for a while.
- Jess made a choice to make a change. The day she made that choice positive things started happening in her life. She knew she had an adult outside the family she could trust, someone who would walk every step of the way with her, and who was talking to the potential she was not yet seeing.
- Jess began to appreciate, now in this supportive environment, that failure is never fatal, but simply an important stepping-stone on her life journey.

> Accept and embrace failure as you work towards your dreams or create your project. The feedback from failure is an essential part of learning. If you haven't failed, it's because you haven't been pushing yourself to reach beyond your current limits. Failure only happens when you step outside your comfort zone and try things that you aren't already skilled at doing.
> —Jeannette Vos[1]

- Jess set achievable, though challenging goals and, as she started achieving them, she began to enjoy life, and achieve much in many

1. Vos, *The Learning Revolution 2.0*.

areas of her life. She appreciated that there are no short-cuts to achieving her potential. Marshall Goldsmith offers a supportive tip:

> Executing the change we hold as a concrete image in our mind is a process. It requires vigilance and diligent self-monitoring. It demands a devotion to rote repetition that we might initially dismiss as simplistic and undignified, even beneath us. More than anything, the process resuscitates an instinct that's been drilled into us as tiny children but slowly dissipates as we learn to enjoy success and fear failure—the importance of trying.[2]

- Jess also found the joy involved in setting and chasing her goals. She extended her goals to life beyond the classroom and became involved in a variety of extracurricular activities—a self-empowering, self-learning journey. As she did so, she started hanging out with positive peers, some of whom probably became lifelong friends.

Jess completed her schooling as a more resilient young woman ready to make a positive difference in her community.

Reflection

Adolescence is about making mistakes and thus the role of all of us in education is to mentor and advise our teenagers on how to cope with the slings and arrows which life throws at them.

—Keith Richardson[3]

---

2. Goldsmith, *Triggers*, 98.
3. Richardson, *Before the Wax Melts*, 97.

6. Overcoming racial prejudice and adversity—Nick's story

Can you remember times during your adolescent years when life seemed to be particularly hard; you jumped one hurdle and then something else occurred and knocked you down; up you got again and something else happened? Small rocks to stumble over, bigger rocks to obstruct your pathway. How did you respond?

Thinking about this led me to some work I did a while ago when I looked at how youth mentoring programs helped young people living in high-risk environments. I created a check-list, if you like, that would be invaluable to anyone mentoring such a young person.

As I thought some more, I was reminded of the years I spent informally mentoring Nick, a teenager from a high-risk, volatile environment in South Africa during the dark days of apartheid. I learnt much about life from many interactions with Nick—an amazing young man who inspired me through the way he overcame adversity—in this cross-cultural, cross-ethnic relationship.

Nick arrived at the school where I was teaching at the time, and was placed in the boarding house of which I was the house leader.

Nick's mother was a domestic servant and he was, in his own words:

> … a young man from the townships who could not even speak English. I was scared but excited. I had to prove myself. Here were the white boys who had privileged positions all their lives. Their primary education was preparing them to be the bosses, whilst mine was to serve their interests. Here I had to compete with them on the same footing. I can tell you it was not easy.

OVERCOMING RACIAL PREJUDICE AND ADVERSITY—NICK'S STORY

Strategies to inspire young people from high-risk environments

There were approximately sixty to seventy boys, aged between twelve and eighteen years, in each boarding house. Nick had to settle quickly, as well as find his way in a large new school. He was a keen sportsman, who played rugby and cricket, though he was particularly fond of football (soccer). Nick attended the school on an academic scholarship, so clearly his potential had been acknowledged by the company which supported him.

There are millions of young people like Nick, and what follows are ten strategies, not in any specific order, which youth mentoring programs (and individual mentors) can adapt to support young people from high-risk environments—in reality, from *any* environment—reach their potential. As I share these strategies, I'll weave Nick's story into the journey.

1. Support and guide young people to realize their potential.

Nick had strong opinions of his own, yet he was prepared to listen, weigh up other viewpoints, and then decide how he would respond. He initially struggled at this new school, which he desperately wanted to attend, for a variety of reasons. Nick wrote:

> Typical of white preconceptions, they thought I was "thick" [stupid] mainly because I was black and I had had a bad education for about seven years. They put me in the bottom groups or "D" classes. Here was the opportunity to prove myself. I knew there were people who believed in me ... through perseverance I climbed up the ladder. Everyone knew there was Nick who was counted among the "boffins" [above average intelligence]. I knew I was not a boffin, just a somebody who had, as our Human Kinetics teacher used to say, "spine, guts, and determination."

Nick seized every opportunity that came his way and sought to make the most of it. My role, initially from a distance, was to encourage him, and support other staff colleagues who taught and coached him, as well as older students in the house who offered further guidance. Nick and I began to converse more as he progressed up the school.

Never underestimate the value of noteworthy adults in the life of a young person. Mentors actively encourage mentees to seek out more important adults to take on the role of non-judgmental cheerleaders in their lives. In this way young people build an ongoing network of positive support around themselves.

2. *Develop positive values in young people.*

It is important to model positive character qualities and values. Paul Browning offers some useful advice, which is relevant to all age groups: "When you understand a person's values, you will have really connected with them and they will feel understood. There are few greater gifts you can offer a person than to demonstrate genuine understanding."[1]

I only realized how important my encouragement of Nick had been after he had left school. He was at university, and I invited him to help me facilitate a non-racial youth empowerment symposium I was organizing. As he was one of the founding participants of these symposia, he had much to offer. He was settling into university life and having to deal with further challenges. After the symposium he sent me a brief note:

> Thank you for the "talk" we had on Saturday night. It's very rare that I actually get someone who I can relate my problems to; but you are there and you certainly revitalized my motivation about my whole career at Varsity [University]. Now what I say to myself: if you can do so much, then why can't I? —and that is what keeps me going.

Through his time at the school, Nick picked up a variety of morals and values and, as he moved on to university, these began to shape his personal value system.

3. *Guide young people towards more reliable attendance at school, further training, or work.*

Although Nick had challenges to deal with at school, at no point did he not want to attend. As he mentions above, he was motivated to "climb the ladder." Nick shared his experiences with a group of students after he had left school:

> They say that if you do not know where you are going, you probably will end up anywhere. You must have set yourself realistic

---

1. Browning, *Principled*, 38.

goals. Have them written down. There is nothing as gratifying as ticking off those goals that you have achieved. You are essentially measuring and awarding yourself. You must have a role model—see yourself as that person and work towards that.

One of my roles had been to guide Nick on the goal setting journey. The goals were his, and we reviewed them every three months during the last two years of his school career. He was focused, had a reason to attend school, and it's along these lines that mentors can often open up discussions with mentees. If young people know there is someone who cares about them, listens to them, and helps them find meaning and purpose in their lives, mindset changes will occur. The fact that Nick was accountable to a non-judgmental cheerleader, motivated him to work hard to achieve his goals.

4. Improve the social and communication skills of young people in relationships with family and extended family, with a focus on behavior, attitudes, and appearance.

What impressed teaching colleagues about Nick was the pride he took in his appearance. My guess is that, having come from a disadvantaged, high-risk environment, Nick seized every moment he could to reach his potential. He knew how important it was to take a pride in his appearance, as we spoke about this at house meetings, had uniform inspections, and we tried to instill in the students at the school the importance of being proud of who they were.

Coach mentees about appearance, body language, and positive communication skills to enhance their options as they move out into the world beyond school.

Nick created a network of support around himself. In addition to his mother, the sponsoring company and some close peers supported him. Nick also had strong support from the family who employed his mother. In addition to teachers, Nick heard messages from a variety of people he trusted who believed in him.

Nick, after leaving school, addressed students at the non-racial school I had moved to as school principal:

> Always think positively about yourself and the situations you find yourself in. You must see problems as opportunities to prove yourself. Believe in yourself and your ability to tackle problems.

Have a positive self-esteem, don't be arrogant. There are no failures in this world, just men and women who don't know how good they are and they are not willing to find out.

5. *Improve the self-image of young people.*

As the non-judgmental cheerleader, the mentor plays a significant role in the life of the mentee. Trust is established and the conversations go to a deeper, more personal level. As I experienced with Nick, young people will share more of their personal feelings, something boys—from my experience—appear to find much harder to do than girls.

Nick shared some of that thinking in the previous point. We talked about goal setting, community service, and lots more. Yet it was the comments Nick shared with students after he had left school that provide some insights into how he developed his self-esteem during his school days:

> Mistakes are learning opportunities. Do not be afraid to make a mistake. You can only learn from your mistakes. As the old Chinese proverb says, "success does not consist in never making mistakes, but in never making the same one a second time." There are many obstacles that you have to overcome; there are people who want you to make mistakes so they can be happy. They channel their energies into making sure you fail. Don't worry about them. They are the real failures, not you.

A smile from a mentor, a brief positive comment that is relaying the message, "I believe in you!" must never be underestimated. Also make sure that your mentee never takes life too seriously. Nick had a great sense of humor, and he and I laughed lots.

6. *Expose young people to positive new experiences such as community involvement, different cultures, and activities.*

One way a mentor can successfully impact the life of a mentee living in a high-risk environment is to take them out of that environment and talk about possibilities. In a way it's a Catch-22 situation. We want our mentees to become pillars of their communities and be the agents of change. Sometimes, as Nick experienced, it's also important to remove oneself from that high-risk environment for a while to discover who we are.

OVERCOMING RACIAL PREJUDICE AND ADVERSITY—NICK'S STORY

Nick took advantage of the activities on offer at school. If he had an issue, it was deciding where to curtail his involvement as he approached his final year at school.

Nick and I firmed up our relationship when he volunteered to attend the first South African Youth Symposium (SAYS) I organized in the late 1980's and which was hosted by our school. The purpose was to bring students and teachers from all cultures and ethnicities in South Africa together, to meet, to break down racial barriers and assumptions, to have fun together, to be challenged by keynote speakers, and then to return to their communities to become positive agents of change preparing themselves and others for the post-apartheid South Africa whenever that would inevitably occur.

The students helped me organize the conference, and were the hosts when students from all around the country arrived in their busloads.

I watched with pride as Nick mixed with anyone and everyone, had lots of fun, joined in the debates, and revealed some significant leadership skills.

What occurred was that Nick was identifying with some deeply held beliefs of mine that he had probably not yet fully appreciated, seen the risks being taken to organize the symposium—visits from the security police during the conference for example, and I was sure my telephone was being tapped—yet, together, we were buying into the vision of what a non-racial South Africa would look, feel, and be like. They were exciting times. Nick and a couple of other students were active helpers and great role models to their peers for a couple of years as I organized these symposia.

7. Enhance a sense of social responsibility in young people.

It is generally agreed by those who teach, coach, or work with young people, that many adolescents live in a world of instant gratification and entitlement, with too much focus on *I* and not enough focus on *We*.

As mentors we can encourage our mentees to think of others. We can explore with them small activities they can do to become positive agents of change in their communities. When they feel accountable to the mentor and supported, mentors are continually amazed at what these young people achieve. I saw many examples of this during my teaching career.

A few years ago, for example, I worked with two students who had a strong sense of responsibility to do something to support cancer research.

They organized a significant fundraising event. My role was to encourage, guide, and help them sort out the financing of the activity, and be present on the day to support them—the authentic cheerleader. They raised over $2000 from the activity and, better still, the next year they mentored two younger students who wanted to carry on what became a legacy started by two of their older peers.

Nick shared this thought with the students he addressed: "Help others if you can. It can be very satisfying when you know that you made another person better off. People will return the favor. Start now while you are still at school and make it a habit!"

8. Improve the conflict resolution skills of young people.

Coach young people how to positively deal with conflicts. This is a significant contribution mentors can make in an adolescent's life journey, especially in the twenty-first century where much communication occurs through social media. Many young people have little understanding about *how* to interpret facial gestures, tone of voice, eye contact, body language, and a process to follow if they are in conflict with someone, and don't wish to see it escalate.

A surprisingly large number of mentors I trained over the years made me aware that they themselves had to improve their own conflict resolution skills. Conflict resolution is a topic I include wherever and whenever I can. Not too long ago I shared the process with a student who was keen to resolve a wobbly relationship issue. She reported later that she had learnt a lot from the experience, and the particular relationship issue had been resolved positively.

One of the most significant conversations I had with Nick occurred as a result of a personal conflict he experienced during his final months at school. He had been an outstanding student leader that year.

One Saturday evening I walked around the boarding house and came across an angry and frustrated Nick. I invited him into my office so we could chat away from his peers and other students.

He told me that he wanted to resign as a student leader.

Earlier that day he had said farewell to one of the black kitchen staff members who was leaving the school. Mason had often played football with Nick and others, so they had a healthy respect for one another. Nick was regarded by some of his peers as fraternizing with Mason, and some unnecessary jibes had been directed at Nick. He had had enough of this type of talk and no longer wished to be in a leadership role. He simply wanted to finish his final exams, leave the school, and head on to university.

Nick and I spent two hours discussing life. We shared stories. We empathized with one another as best as we could. Significantly, Nick felt listened to, respected and cared for, and he made a point of coming to see me during the following week to thank me for the time we had spent chatting.

Nick did not step down as a leader. I'd like to think that the discussion we had that evening gave him tools he could use in life beyond school whenever conflicts occurred within his life, and in his workplace.

9. *Encourage young people to make positive life choices.*

The conversation Nick and I had that Saturday evening included a lengthy discussion about positive life choices, the focus also on how, as individuals, we become positive people of influence in our communities. The mentor takes on the role of Devil's Advocate. I usually tell students that I am taking on that role and, in case they don't understand the term, I explain my role.

Nick shared his experiences with students after he had left school and made a particularly telling point:

> Do away with an inferiority complex. I have heard some people say that blacks have short hair because they have short brains. They say that is the reason why some of our people have hair extensions or use hair straighteners or grow dreadlocks, so they can be clever. Well, that is not true. We are very good. We just have not had the opportunity. We must get out of that mentality that "The baas [white boss] is always right." Your color does not determine your intelligence. You are just as good as everyone else. Do not be afraid to challenge authority, but do it the right way. Eventually they will listen to you.

The mentor, remember, will often speak to the potential the mentee might not see. That's another reason why a mentor must *never quit* the mentoring relationship, no matter how challenging things might be.

10. *Help young people to become self-sufficient, productive citizens.*

This can be a key personal goal every mentor of an adolescent sets for themselves as they enter a mentoring relationship.

Have discussions about different career pathways, what being a responsible citizen involves, and the importance of managing finances. Encourage creativity, innovation, and entrepreneurial thinking. Encourage your mentee to take non-life-threatening risks, and then be there for them if they fail while attempting something that has moved them out of their comfort zone.

By the time Nick left school he had become a self-sufficient, responsible, and productive young man who had identified his strengths.

After he had left school, Nick sent me this note:

> Thank you for being a good house leader who is highly considerate of all the members of the House. You have been particularly good to me, giving me advice when I needed it and you kept me going in depressing times. That is why my days in the House will remain in my memory forever.

Nick went to university and gained a Business Degree with Honors, and eventually was appointed to a management position in the company in which he worked. Sadly, his life was cut short by illness when he was in his early forties.

These, then, are ten possible strategies youth mentoring programs can adapt to support young people living in high-risk environments reach their potential. As a result of their experiences, many of these young people might have built a wall around themselves and find it difficult to be vulnerable. Qualities like empathy, sensitivity, and even more listening are required from a mentor. Throw in a few laughs where and when appropriate—Nick, remember, had a fantastic sense of humor—consistently turn up for meetings, and a mentor will eventually connect with a mentee at a deeper level. Mentoring experts Carla Herrera and Michael Garringer offer some supportive words of wisdom to mentors:

> As a mentor you can be a major asset in helping youth move from surviving to *thriving* by helping them turn spaces shaped by oppression, bias, prejudice, and injustices into spaces rooted in liberation, empowerment, belonging and equity.[2]

I have shared parts of Nick's story. I was incredibly proud when he stood in front of my school's assembly, shortly after he had graduated from university, and shared his experiences in an address entitled: "Brace Yourself! It's Tough out There!"

2. Herrera and Garringer, *Becoming a Better Mentor*.

It's therefore appropriate that Nick has the final word:

> There is a Zulu saying, "Umuntu ngumuntu ngabantu." This is a version of "No Man is an Island," and actually means: "a person is a person through other persons." We do not have to compete against each other all the time. Do not climb on the heads of your brothers and sisters to get to the top. If you do that, you must remember that "the higher you are, the harder you fall." All these things that I have mentioned [in this address] are possible because of God. Remember that God only helps those who help themselves. You must also believe in yourself to make things happen. No one is going to make them happen for you. As one bumper sticker read, "The only free lunch is found in a mouse trap." Get advice from other people. Have a goal and, remember, the road to success is always under construction.

Reflection

When all youths—not only youths from high-risk environments—are provided with an atmosphere that treats them as significant, they inevitably become more interested in their own positive transformation. Ex-gang member Rena, who has transformed her life and her attitude through service, epitomized this phenomenon when she explained: "When I discovered that people cared about me—that they believed in my potential as a leader, that they wanted me to succeed—that changed my life. Having someone over your shoulder telling you that you are powerful and that even you can make a difference in your community is compelling."

—Author Unknown

7. Social media and youth—Brittany's and Sarah's stories

Sixteen-year-old Brittany shared with me some of the challenging issues she faced with her best friend. There was a conflict that needed to be resolved. Brittany was confused. She was finding the gossip and friendship issues, which were also being played out on social media platforms, draining. We shared some strategies she could use to help her through those challenges. Brittany needed to understand that, when approached with an open and positive mind, it is possible to look at conflict as having a *positive* value. When handled constructively, conflict can help us to

- learn new problems;
- build better and more durable relationships;
- learn more about ourselves and others, including the style of behavior we follow when dealing with conflicts.

Brittany, like most young people, wanted to belong to a peer group. This led to a discussion about creating a number of circles of friends with whom she could interact, rather than become isolated if she had a setback with someone in one particular circle, and found herself on the outside.

Brittany decided to trust me. Her stress and anxiety levels decreased as a result of the communication we had, and the fact that she knew I was not sitting in judgment on her, and was encouraging her to be the "real" Brittany. She and her friend agreed to disagree on their issue, and the friendship got back on track over a period of time.

All this had me thinking about young people and the impact that social media, indeed, the online world might have on any adolescent who struggles to fit in. I remembered sixteen-year-old Blake sharing the number of hours he was spending online after school and during weekends—an unhealthy scenario which his parents did nothing about. Fifteen-year-old Mia became embroiled in relationship issues because of messages she shared on her cellphone.

British scientist, writer, broadcaster, and speaker Baroness Susan Greenfield shared thoughts about what we can see in adolescents, as they explore social media and the internet: "... an all too human mind-set amplified in all its frailty and vulnerability, craving attention as a unique individual and, at the same time, paradoxically, needing desperately to belong and to be embraced within a collective identity and mind-set."[1]

Possible signs of internet addiction

The CRC Health Group is the largest provider of specialized mental and behavioral health care in the USA. They shared thoughts about a number of behavioral and physiological indicators that "might" suggest an adolescent has an internet addiction:

- most non-school hours are spent on the computer playing video games;
- falling asleep in school;
- falling behind with assessments and assignments;
- worsening grades, test, or exam results;
- lying about computer or video game use;
- choosing to use the computer, or play video games rather than see friends;
- dropping out of other social groups such as clubs, sports, or youth groups;
- being irritable when not playing a video game, or not on the computer;
- carpal tunnel syndrome—joint pain in fingers, hands and wrists—from repetitive motions that come with excessive keyboard use;
- insomnia;
- skipping food in order to remain online;
- neglecting personal hygiene in order to remain online;
- headaches, back pain, and neck pain;
- dry eyes and vision problems.

1. Greenfield, *Mind Change*.

SECTION THREE: MENTORING IN ACTION

Of course, we are looking for *persistent* issues such as a student falling asleep in class. It might be because they worked most of the night on a project, or some other family related matter. However, if there is a pattern of the student sleeping in class more regularly, that should raise alarm bells, and lead to a discussion with the student about the choices they are making linked to their wellbeing.

Fifteen-year-old Sarah appeared to be developing anxiety issues and, from all accounts, displayed signs of disengaging from some activities she had been involved in on a regular basis. Self-image? Sense of belonging issues? Internet issues?

I never heard Sarah's full story. She was in all probability a normal adolescent confronting a time of confusion in her life. But what if Sarah had no one to talk to, or didn't feel she had anyone she could trust to share these deeper feelings? She might easily retreat to the online world, or join questionable chat rooms. Her anxiety levels "might" also increase and this would probably negatively impact her academic studies.

At times like these, when one is aware of a student possibly becoming drawn into the world of online addiction, or withdrawing from their social group, as examples, that non-judgmental wise adult guide on the side has an important role to play in the adolescent's life. I was able to take on that role for a short season of Sarah's school journey as she successfully worked through her issues.

If an adult can have a conversation with the young person, listening, showing empathy, and being non-judgmental, that young person "might" hesitantly, at first, allow the adult into their lives. No matter what occurs, rest assured that the young person *will be listening*, even if every facial gesture, the body language, tone of voice, and lack of eye contact suggests otherwise. Seize the opportunity and start sowing the seeds underpinning the spirit of mentoring:

- Chat about the young person's wellbeing and how they can look after themselves physically by following a healthy diet—where this is possible—and doing their best to have nine hours sleep *every* night. Jeannette Vos has noted: "The area most often forgotten in schooling and the workplace is that the brain and mind must be nurtured through proper nutrition. Food impacts your mood (mind health) and the wiring of your brain."[2]

---

2. Vos, *The Learning Revolution 2.0*.

- Share with them how they can undertake a self-learning and self-empowering journey as they take control of their lives. They can set personal best goals and work towards achieving them one small step at a time. Initially encourage the student to set fairly simple goals that you believe they can easily achieve. Once they have tasted success, they are likely to step up and set more challenging goals—with your non-judgmental support and encouragement—that will take them out of their comfort zones.

- Focus on what they want with regard to their relationships, and help them create strategies to develop meaningful relationships, a process that takes time. Encourage the young person to take time away from the internet and social media, and engage in discussions about their feelings, or their challenging issues with someone who will listen to them, someone they are prepared to trust—a relative (grandparents are often brilliant in this area), a positive peer, a teacher, a coach, or a mentor.

Brittany's and Sarah's stories remind me of other strategies that can be used to show care and support for others. In a school, for example, a mixed-age Vertical Tutoring System (see Appendix 3) has older students offering positive peer support to younger students who might be unwell or struggling for a variety of reasons. They could also adapt an effective strategy used with older students, and shared by experienced educators Magdalena Brzezinska and Edward Cromarty:

> At the beginning of a synchronous session, each student was asked to select an emoji that would reflect individual feelings and attitudes. The instructor commented on the emojis in real time, in a sensitive, empathetic, non-judgmental way. When a "sick" or "unwell" emoji appeared, the students would be encouraged to support the ill-disposed peer. The support could be expressed by reacting to the emoji with a heart, sending the peer a private message, or by individually selecting an alternative manner of assistance. That was one of the elements of the culture of mindfulness and care being recreated online.[3]

---

3. Brzezinska and Cromarty, *Emergency Remote Teaching*, 39.

Reflection

You usually see in others what you expect to see. If you constantly expect and see good things in others, it is much easier to maintain a positive attitude ... People generally rise to meet your level of expectation. If you treat them positively, they tend to treat you the same way. If you expect them to get the job done and you show the confidence in them, they usually succeed. No matter what the circumstances, positive people see opportunities everywhere.

—Author unknown

8. Swimming the English Channel—eight life lessons from Trent Grimsey's story

Have you ever chased a dream and succeeded in reaching it?

I remember, as a fifteen-year-old, how I chased a dream to represent my state running cross-country, the sacrifices I made, the hard yards I put into training, and the wonderful feeling of accomplishment when I was selected for the state team at the end of my most successful cross-country season. I then achieved sixth place in the inter-state race to cap off a great season.

Nothing could be achieved without setting some personal best goals and having the support of family and coaches. Ed Bowers writes: "Goals direct the decisions we make, the actions we take, and ultimately, the direction our lives take. Therefore, it is critical that mentors are intentional in providing goal support to their mentees."[1]

Trent Grimsey's story reminded me of those days, as well as the importance of sharing one's stories with young people. They love true stories.

A few years ago, I listened to Trent, at that time the current world record holder of the English Channel swim, share his story with a group of impressionable young students. Trent described how, as an average swimmer (in his opinion) he had achieved many medals, yet narrowly missed out on selection for the 2008 Australian Olympic Team.

Wondering what he should do to stay motivated, Trent decided to swim the English Channel, not just to complete the swim, but to break the world record.

There are at least eight lifelong lessons, and mentoring strategies to be learned from Trent's experience planning and swimming the English

1. Bowers, *Becoming a Better Mentor.*

Channel, which can be shared to inspire a young person to reach their potential.

1. *Always have a clear goal and share it with someone you trust.* Trent firmly believed that, with a sense of purpose, it was easier to stay motivated and inspired, and to live a positive life. As a swimmer, he needed a coach he could trust, who was knowledgeable about long-distance swimming, someone who believed in him, and what he set out to achieve; and someone who would support him the whole way. During the actual Channel swim Trent's coach appears to have been a key figure in keeping Trent motivated and focused on achieving his goal.

2. *Thorough planning and preparation.* The planning and preparation during the *three years* that Trent dedicated to his English Channel swim were incredible. He decided to study the then world record holder, Bulgarian Peter Stoychev, trying to get inside his brain and fully understand his preparation. Trent found out which boat Peter had used to escort him across the Channel and booked the same boat three years in advance. Trent swam long distance races against Peter to learn as much as he could about him. Wherever Trent went, he took down copious notes, determined that his preparation for the Channel swim would be the best it possibly could be.

3. *Watch your diet and nutrition.* Trent needed to be supremely fit when he attempted the swim, which involved careful planning of his diet, when he would eat or drink during the Channel swim, and in the time leading up to the swim. His planning was meticulous. A healthy lifestyle is important if we wish to reach our potential.

4. *Be teachable.* One of the messages that came across loud and clear was the importance of being teachable. Trent spent hours researching all sorts of things—including the tides, winds, and currents—as he planned the English Channel swim. He sought the advice and opinions of others whenever he could find the people who might help him achieve his goal. That included discussions with the escort boat captain who had great knowledge of the currents. Trent also studied Peter Stoychev's swimming style, eager to pick up as many tips as possible from the world record holder.

5. *Extend yourself.* Trent shared some stories of his swimming career when he would swim more training laps than his rivals, and do more exercises out of the pool than his rivals, as well as examples of how he became better and better as an athlete. While it was tough work, the fact that he was doing that little bit extra proved to be important motivation as he chased his dream. What he might have lacked in talent, when compared to his closest rivals, he more than made up with hard work.

6. *Persevere.* Trent stressed a few times the importance of persevering and not quitting when his body, his whole being was saying, "quit!" "You'll get a second wind and so don't quit," Trent told the students. A powerful message for the life journey.

7. *Stay focused.* Trent stressed the importance of staying focused on attaining the goal at all times. During the actual swim he had to focus on all the strategies planned with his coach to ensure he achieved his goal.

8. *Believe in yourself.* This was another powerful message Trent shared. There was no arrogance as he shared his belief that, if one trains hard, prepares hard, and lives a healthy lifestyle, dreams can be achieved. Trent spoke of how he woke up the morning of his English Channel swim in a positive head space. He believed he would be breaking the record as he was in such good physical and mental shape.

In 2012 Trent broke the world record for the cross-channel fastest solo swim by two minutes. After Trent retired, he trained long-distance swimmers, an effective way to pass on a legacy.

Trent's humility and courage, together with a delightful sense of humor, were three further stand-out qualities evident as he shared his story.

How will a mentor know if the young person they are walking alongside is making progress?

When the goal setting journey is effective, you will observe a young person who has

- a sense of pride and self-worth;
- greater knowledge and experience (focus on topics of their interest);
- greater independence (and the ability to make good choices);
- a stronger ability to respond to failures constructively and positively;
- a greater tolerance of responsible risk-taking.

Reflection

Knowing how to set realistic, attainable goals is a skill, but it is also a state of mind. You have to have enough confidence in yourself to know that you can reach the goal you set in order to take the risk of trying for it. And every accomplished objective, in turn, increases your faith in yourself and makes it easier to reach for the bigger prizes. It is important to keep this in mind as you go about encouraging your mentee to set goals. Find out what the young person dreams about, and then discuss how you can break down the dream into several smaller objectives that build on each other ... The process of working toward a major goal will help him or her to develop an essential life skill and a few successes will help boost his or her confidence as he or she makes plans and prepares for the future.

—Thomas W. Dortch Jr[2]

---

2. Dortch, *The Miracles of Mentoring*.

9. Strategies and tips to guide teenagers how to overcome adversity—Colin's story

What was your worst school experience as a teenager and how did you overcome it?

Sixteen-year-old Colin, only average both academically and as a sportsman, made one crucial error when he was caught in possession of marijuana, and was asked to leave the school.

His world began to fall apart, but he responded to support and encouragement from his sports coach, as well as his parents, enrolled at another school closer to home, and performed successfully in all aspects of school life, vowing never to experiment with drugs again.

Negative peer pressure had been Colin's downfall.

However, this was not an easy time for Colin, as he came to terms with a choice he had made. He had to learn how his choice determined his future.

Reflecting on Colin's journey, I recall six key decisions Colin made that helped him bounce back from adversity.

1. At first Colin did not want to engage with anyone. He was embarrassed to speak to me (the sports coach) as he felt he had let both the team and me down. He—and his parents—felt he had been treated unfairly, as he had never been in trouble at school before. Then he *agreed to talk*.

2. Colin *chose* to speak to me. I listened as he described what had happened. Decisions had been taken by school authorities, and there was nothing I could do about this. Colin reluctantly understood this. We were *honest* with each other. Colin was learning how and when to be vulnerable, and I was validating his courage and willingness to explore new options.

3. Colin then had to decide what the way ahead would look like. He explored his *options*. A part of him wanted to give up completely, drop out of school, and find any job. I encouraged him to look at other possibilities, and suggested that he had much untapped potential.

4. Colin realized that the choices he made would define his future, and he could blame no one else for these choices. He chose to *change his attitude*, learn from the experience and enroll in another school. This took courage.

5. Colin's parents and I moved alongside him to support him as he settled into the new school. Fortunately, he knew a few students, and his sport also helped him become quickly accepted. He had to *deal with the peer pressure*, as it did not take long for other students to find out what had happened to Colin prior to arriving at his new school. Colin's parents wrote: "Thank you for being such an understanding friend to Colin and a support to us. When one hits the bottom, it is good to know that there is a friend who cares."

6. Colin *chose not to quit*. He took a new, *positive attitude* into his new school and, within a few months, was chasing new goals and making excellent progress. Colin was a young man of few words. I was touched when he sent me this note: "Thank you for all you have done to help me as a master and as a friend. You have helped me to make the right decisions about my education."

Perhaps the *defining moment* for Colin was when he came to understand that we all experience failure in life. Rather than blame others for our poor decisions, we take ownership of those decisions, learn from these temporary setbacks and move on, determined to fulfil our potential.

When teenagers allow other, more experienced adults to guide them along the life journey, they find reassurance, as they appreciate that they are not walking alone. These adults are their non-judgmental cheerleaders and, most important, they come to understand that these people believe in them, and will guide them through confusing and challenging times.

How did you work through that tough time at school? You have a story to share with a young person.

Reflection

Few journalists understand that every adolescent seeks to test boundaries of acceptable behavior, and boundaries of relationships with authority, the opposite sex and peers. Issues like these need to be resolved in a non-threatening atmosphere behind closed doors.

What really helps on the journey of adolescence is if every boy has a role model and mentor who can nudge him back gently from that boundary ...

—Keith Richardson[1]

---

1. Richardson, *Before the Wax Melts*, 267.

10. How to support a teenager who wants to drop out of school

Were there any times during your adolescent years when you felt like dropping out of school? Personal issues clouded your judgment, perhaps? Or you felt that you had no one to turn to? Or you feared leaving school because you had no idea what career to follow?

We have no idea what lies around the corner later today, tomorrow, next week, next month, or next year. It is unknown territory especially for our young people who continually hear that many of today's jobs will disappear, yet no one knows with certainty what the future job market will look like.

The storm clouds of confusion are threatening and never seem to move along.

Over the years I have spent time with young people who struggled with issues like these for a variety of reasons. Some have wanted to give up completely and leave school, believing that they can find a job, and that is all that matters.

There will be a story behind these feelings, as there always is and, if you are in a mentoring role, you can discern what is going on as you and your mentee connect and establish a trusting and meaningful relationship. Be patient, as this might take some time.

Often young people need encouragement to share what is on their mind knowing that they will not be judged. They need reassurance that their current state of confusion is experienced by an overwhelming number of teenagers at a variety of times during the adolescent journey.

There are occasions when they might need a reality check before they make a decision, such as dropping out of school, which they might regret for many years.

Truancy often points to bigger issues going on in a young person's life. Each instance of truancy will be different. Never be afraid to ask for assistance from someone more experienced if you are feeling the issues are more complex, and you are not comfortable trying to work through them alone.

Once your mentee is more relaxed communicating with you and starts sharing at a deeper level, you can chat about the social and economic costs of dropping out of school, work, or further training (as applicable).

You can, with the permission of your mentee, take on the role of Devil's Advocate which will allow you to force your mentee to think seriously about any choices with potentially serious long-term consequences.

Discuss all the long-term options for your mentee. What options will remain open if they leave school before being ready to do so? Or, if they terminate a job without adequate notice? Or, give up a training course without completing it?

A Seven Steps Strategy

You might find this Seven Steps Strategy helpful in shaping any discussions:

1. Stop. Think about the problem. Discuss it. Validate the person for having the courage and willingness to be vulnerable, and to share deeper thoughts and feelings.
2. What are some possible choices?
3. Choose *one* of these options.
4. Write it down. This is often a great opportunity to launch into a goal setting strategy.
5. Put it into action within an agreed, sensible, given time.
6. Arrange a time for follow-up together to assess how things are progressing.
7. At the follow-up, discuss how the chosen option worked. Celebrate the small victories as they are achieved.

The key is to see yourself as the non-judgmental cheerleader who never quits on your mentee. Some days this might seem hard yet, if you persevere, you might suddenly experience your mentee's "aha!" moment when they seem to have discovered a way forward. The storm clouds have gone and the sun is shining again. This could lead to new thinking, a desire for more personal and realistic goals, and the beginning of a whole new life journey.

Use these small steps with an abundance of encouragement as you both look positively into the unknown future, and create life changing moments.

This is the spirit of mentoring.

Reflection

[Mentoring] is a process of opening our lives to others; of sharing our lives with others; a process of living for the next generation.

—Ron Lee Davis

11. Handling the highs and lows of stress

How well did you handle stress as a teenager? The times when your friends annoyed you? A family member annoyed you? You had to prepare for a test, or an exam? A teacher humiliated you in front of peers? You were running late for an appointment? You had to meet a deadline? You had been rejected three times already in your search for a part-time job and you really needed the cash? You were waiting for an interview and feeling so stressed about it, or you were having the interview and finding it quite a stressful experience? You were in a family where there was abuse of some kind going on?

Most of us deal with a variety of stressful situations almost daily. There is the positive stress, when we have those butterfly feelings prior to performing somewhere, or take part in a drama, or sports performance for which we have practiced hard. There is the negative stress, examples of which are given above. I have known of many people, young and old, who turn to illegal drugs, alcohol, or some other substance when they feel stressed. This is only a temporary solution to their feelings. It will probably only make things worse judging from all the recent brain research which suggests that adolescents who mess with drugs, get involved in binge drinking and other antisocial behavior activities, could do permanent brain damage while the brain develops.

I have worked with many young people who have had to deal with stressful situations. One successful strategy most learned quite quickly was that when they were organized, and did some proper planning—with my help initially—they reduced the amount of stress in their lives. I know that's true from personal experience.

If there were relationship issues causing stress, it was important for them to find someone they trusted with whom they could share their feelings. This is a positive way to deal with stress and, of course, it became obvious that they should avoid drugs, not abuse alcohol—preferably not touch alcohol until they were legally allowed to do so—or become violent towards anyone, or anything.

Helen Street offers some wise words for those working with young people:

> Build positive relationships with children by managing your own stress effectively (adult wellbeing is the foundation of both effective parenting and effective teaching). And, just as importantly, take an active interest in the feelings and aspirations of the children in your care.[1]

Stress-less tips

The following stress-less tips have always been a great encouragement and help to me, especially because they were shared by one of my mentors. He made many sacrifices in his life, sometimes at great personal cost, though he was an excellent role model, always on time for meetings, always carrying out his commitments and, no matter what the situation might be, he had a fantastic sense of humor.

- Follow a healthy diet.
- Don't abuse substances (drugs) or become involved in inappropriate sexual behavior.
- Avoid smoking (or vaping).
- Drink only a modest amount of alcohol [when you are legally allowed to do so], or preferably none at all.
- Be effective in your goal getting, planning, and coping with day-to-day affairs.
- Get proper and regular exercise.
- Have regular and structured time for relaxation.
- Pray and take time to think about, or reflect on life.

Educators Magdalena Brzezinska and Edward Cromarty share a useful supportive strategy to move alongside older students and young adults who might be struggling for a variety of reasons:

---

1. Street, *Better Than OK*, 39.

... constant empathy and support were conveyed by asking students how they were doing, inquiring (both in person and in writing) if they needed assistance, expressing support for their ongoing efforts, and informing them of sources of institutional help and assistance, such as national and self-governmental programs to fight depression.[2]

Reflection

When you see young kids feeling good about themselves and becoming more self-reliant, you know you're onto something. They see that you can have dreams and can aspire to achieve them. They learn that there are people who care and are willing to work to help them reach their dreams ... We help young people get through the "glass walls" in this country—the barriers between racial, religious and cultural groups. We need to break down these walls and show that there are more similarities than differences. Mentoring is a real-life example of people coming together for the common good ... Your impact has to go beyond immediate family and friends. As a mentor, you get to pass the baton, to shape and influence another human being. It doesn't get a whole lot better than that.

—Harry L. Coaxum

---

2. Brzezinska and Cromarty, *Emergency Remote Teaching*, 38.

12. Learning to overcome obstacles with a positive attitude—true stories

Effective mentors guide and coach their mentees to understand that becoming a winner means achieving greatness, or developing into the best person they can be, and reaching their unique potential. It is not simply about being better than anyone else. It includes taking responsibility for their choices, and becoming accountable for their actions.

If they choose to be a winner and make the most of their abilities, they can think positively, and seek positive people to influence them.

It's about being a great team player, learning how to solve problems, being creative and innovative, perhaps even developing some entrepreneurial skills.

A winner expects success and does not say *I can't!* when the going gets tough.

There are many stories of people who have overcome obstacles on the way to fulfilling their potential. Here are a few examples for mentors to discuss with their mentees at an appropriate time. Many of these are ordinary people.

- *Adrian Kenny* returned to New Zealand from Europe in 1991 with no money and many debts. He started mowing lawns and soon built a business from his lawn mowing business. He established the Green Acres Franchise group which won many awards. Over 600 Green Acres franchisees emerged, including a car valet service, a home cleaning service, a carpet cleaning service, and a dog grooming service.
- Canadian *Terry Fox* had his cancer-ridden leg amputated. He decided to run from coast to coast to raise $1 million for cancer research. The cancer invaded his lungs, forcing him to stop half way. His efforts

and the foundation he pioneered raised over $20 million for cancer research.

- *Ann Bancroft* overcame a learning disability to become the first woman to travel to the North Pole in 1986. In 1992 and 1993 she also became the first woman to lead an all-women dog-sled team to the South Pole.

- Australian *Katrina Webb* discovered at the age of eighteen, while on a netball scholarship at the Australian Institute of Sport, that she had a mild case of Cerebral Palsy. Courageously she tackled her disability and competed at the 1996 Paralympic Games in Atlanta where she won gold medals in the 100 and 200 meters, and a silver medal in the long jump. She won more medals in the Sydney 2000 Paralympic Games, and at the 2004 Paralympic Games in Athens.

- American *Jody Williams* began the International Campaign to ban Land Mines (ICBL) in 1991. As a result of her courageous and inspiring efforts a 1997 Land Mine Ban Treaty in Ottawa was signed, and she was awarded the Nobel Peace Prize in the same year for the ICBL's efforts. In 2004 Forbes Magazine named her one of the most powerful women in the world.

- *Oprah Winfrey* overcame many personal difficulties as a result of child abuse and, aged seventeen, began her television career. She became the first African-American woman to become a billionaire. Her corporate mission was clearly spelt out for the Oprah Winfrey Show: "... to use television to transform people's lives, to make viewers see themselves differently and to bring happiness and a sense of fulfilment into every home."

- Many women have had to overcome strong opposition and many difficulties in their lives, yet have gone on to inspire millions of people throughout the world because of their courageous efforts. They include, *Gladys Aylward*, missionary to China; *JK Rowling*, author (Harry Potter series); *Joan of Arc*, fifteenth century national French heroine; *Emily Pankhurst*, woman's suffragette movement; *Kelly Holmes*, gold medal winner at the 2004 Athens Olympics; *Helen Keller*, born blind and deaf, American author, activist and lecturer.

- German composer *Ludwig van Beethoven* handled the violin awkwardly and preferred playing his own compositions, which his teacher described as hopeless. By the age of forty-six Beethoven was completely deaf. He went on to write his greatest music, including five symphonies.

- New Zealander *Bruce McLaren* died while testing his motor racing car in England at the age of thirty-two. He had at one time been the number two driver in the world for ten years. He had overcome a disease, which had affected his hip since the age of nine, to pursue his love of motor cars. Team McLaren has been one of the most successful teams in world motor sport since it appeared in 1966—what a legacy.

- The following people had learning disabilities, yet were not stopped from pursuing and achieving their dreams: *John Lennon*, singer, musician, songwriter (one of the Beatles); *Whoopi Goldberg*, actress and comedian; *Winston Churchill*, Prime Minister of Great Britain; *Tom Cruise*, actor; *Cher*, singer, actress; *Bill Wilson*, founder of Alcoholics Anonymous; *Keira Knightly*, actress; *Jamie Oliver*, chef; *Jewel*, singer.

- In 1952 *Edmund Hillary* attempted to climb Mount Everest, at 29,000 feet the highest mountain in the world. He failed. Addressing a group in England a few weeks later, it is said that New Zealander Hillary walked to the edge of the stage, made a fist, and pointed at a picture of Everest and said: "Mount Everest, you beat me the first time, but I'll beat you the next time because you've grown all you are going to grow." On May 29 1953 Hillary and his Nepali-Indian Sherpa mountaineer guide *Tensing Norgay* became the first people to reach its summit.

- American physicist *Chester Carlson* was a young inventor who unsuccessfully took an idea to twenty corporations during the 1940s. After seven years of rejections, the small Haloid company in New York purchased the rights to his electrostatic paper-copying process. Haloid would eventually become Xerox Corporation. The photocopier machine was born.

- American *Henry Ford* went broke five times before he finally succeeded in the motor car industry, which is perhaps a reason he said: "Failure is only the opportunity to begin again more intelligently." After growing up on a farm, he worked as a mechanic, then as a fire fighter in the Detroit Edison Company where he later became chief engineer. Ultimately, he founded Ford Motor Company. He observed, "Nothing is particularly hard if you divide it into small jobs."

- *Sylvester Stallone* wrote the script for *Rocky* in three-and-a-half days, inspired by a boxing fight he watched on television. Most producers turned him down, especially when he said he had to take the lead in the film. Finally, the film was produced. *Rocky* grossed more than $100 million, with Stallone playing the lead role.
- American *Walt Disney* was fired by a newspaper for lack of ideas. He went bankrupt several times before he developed his successful animated movie studio and built Disneyland. Walt Disney was a creative man always envisioning what could be achieved. He sought out excellence. His motto was: "If you can dream it, you can have it!"

Reflection

Mentors are encouragers. They demonstrate the mentor's spirit … You might say that their attributes, indeed their lives, bear witness to transcendent realities. For instance, they are virtuous—good stewards of their own and the greater good. They are trusting and trustworthy—faithful to a constant set of superordinate values. They are people lovers, and unabashed lovers of life. They are empathetic and non-judgmental—we feel that our mentors accept us unconditionally. They are also authentic. Relying on an internal compass, they figure out how to be themselves despite obstacles or shifting circumstances.

—Marsha Sinetar[1]

---

1. Sinetar, *The Mentor's Spirit*.

13. Mentoring moments—through the lens of young people

What would you have liked a significant adult in your life to have said to you when you were an adolescent?

Here is a list of comments some adult mentor trainees shared with me in response to this question as they reflected on a person who had a significant influence during their teenage years. The power behind these short sentences is significant, especially when shared by an authentic mentor.

"I know that you can do it!"

"Pursue your dreams and never give up on that prize."

"I think you're really brave being able to cope on your own."

"Keep doing what you're doing. Stay optimistic."

"I know you are capable of achieving anything you set out to do in your life."

"You have an optimistic and very positive outlook on life."

"Believe in yourself. You have all the capabilities."

"People need to see and read what you have to say."

"You really will get there in the end if you keep working at it."

"I truly believe that you will do an amazing job of it."

"I really admire the way you persevere and encourage others constantly."

"I believe in you! And you can do it!"

"You are a very special person and you are okay just the way you are."

"You have a beautiful smile and you make me very happy."

"I'm so proud of you!"

"I believe that whatever you set your mind to you will achieve. I will be your biggest supporter. I will encourage and advise you. Most of all, I will celebrate with you!"

Every message communicates a word of "hope" and encouragement. During the mentoring journey it is important for mentors to pause on occasions, and reflect on the quality of the messages their mentees hear in their interactions with their mentors.

As mentors, be encouraged by the words of Archbishop Desmond Tutu, Nobel Peace Prize winner: "Do your little bit of good where you are; it's those little bits of good put together that overwhelm the world."

Mentees share thoughts about their mentors

It is also helpful to reflect on what mentees have said about their mentors to help us understand what these young people need from their non-judgmental cheerleaders.

You will hear a variety of comments. The one that I have heard the most is: "My mentor never quits on me!"

Here are some of the comments made by young people about their volunteer adult mentors, and the mentoring experience in youth mentoring programs with which I have been linked.

"I admired my mentor."

"We had fun together."

"She accepted me where I was."

"… a consistent, stable person in my life."

"A person of character, trustworthy."

"Affirming."

"We enjoyed a natural and positive relationship."

"He believed in me."

"He saw the potential in me which I could not see."

"She never seemed to judge me."

"I knew my mentor wasn't perfect, and that didn't matter."

"He saw me as a person of value."

"He cared for me."

"She let me go at my pace, and I really appreciated that."

"A helping hand when I was struggling."

"He was genuine."

As should be clear from most of the comments above, the relationship involves an empathetic attitude, the mentor knowing when to let go, and how to move at the pace of the mentee. This is significant in the establishment of a meaningful, developmental mentoring relationship.

Fifteen-year-old students reflected briefly on their school-based mentoring experiences and wrote these comments. Note the variety of responses. Every mentee is unique.

"Helped me with job opportunities e.g., work experience."

"She has helped me write my resume. She organized work experience. Good rapport."

"She has helped me with a lot of things ... having someone to talk to."

"He has been there if I needed to talk ... make it [the mentoring program] last longer."

"She has taught me to control my anger and shown the importance of a good career."

A key function of mentors is to assist their mentees to apply what they learn in school, or the workplace to everyday life. Provide opportunities to explore new situations, places, and cultures, move out of their comfort zone, and you broaden your mentees' knowledge, and assist them to translate life experiences into meaningful learning opportunities.

Marc Freedman said: "Mentoring is mostly about small victories and subtle changes."[1] Mentors continually look for those small moments when they can catch a young person doing something good, and can genuinely affirm their "efforts."

Supportive words from mentoring experts Carla Herrera and Michael Garringer: "The role of a mentor is unique, as it speaks to a relationship that is grounded not only in love, but also in common purpose and with an eye to the future."[2]

Support and inspire your mentees to enter more meaningful relationships with peers and other adults in the future as you forge a positive and meaningful relationship with them, and take that spirit of optimism into the relationship. Marshall Goldsmith writes:

---

1. Freedman, *The Kindness*, 95.
2. Herrera and Garringer, *Becoming a Better Mentor*.

Optimism—not only feeling it inside but showing it on the outside—is a magic move. People are automatically drawn to the confident individual who believes everything will work out. They want to be led [mentored] by this person. They'll work overtime to help this person succeed. Optimism almost makes the change process a self-fulfilling prophecy.[3]

Reflection

A person with high self-efficacy believes they can reach their goal and they take the steps required to make it happen. They work harder. They raise their hands more. They ask questions. They practice, get it wrong, and try again.

—Carmine Gallo[4]

---

3. Goldsmith, *Triggers,* 101.
4. Gallo, *The Storyteller's Secret.*

SECTION FOUR

Preparing young people for the world of work during the mentoring journey

This section offers strategies and tips to anyone working with adolescents and young adults who, at some point, will show an interest in obtaining casual work, a part-time job, or a full-time job depending on their personal circumstances. There is more information online, which mentors can sift through with the young person they guide. The content of this section is deliberately straightforward, a reminder that, for a young person entering the workplace for the first time, they are likely to experience a mixture of anxiety, apprehension, and excitement. There are strategies and tips to help employers of young people, and the section is completed with true stories portraying the power of the spirit of mentoring in a variety of settings.

If you're not certain of the value of mentorship, think of how many elite athletes or professional sports teams train without a coach. Zero. How many of your favorite films are made without a producer or director? Zero. How many of the best schools in the world function without teachers? Zero. It's safe to say that every great leader, in any field, first had a great mentor. Finding a mentor who inspires and guides your growth is a life-changing experience. Mentors help us to transcend the limits, or perceived limits, of our abilities. A mentor can be anyone who teaches us and helps us to grow in ways we couldn't have on our own.

—Tina Turner[1]

---

1. Turner, *Happiness Becomes You*, 100.

1. Career thoughts before entering the world of work

Most teenagers are asking themselves this question: What should I do if I am unsure about what I would like to do when I finish school?

Here are some questions a mentor can discuss with their mentee.

1. What do I want from a job? That is, do I want to:

   - work with other people, or by myself?
   - work outdoors, or indoors?
   - sit at a desk, or be physically active?

2. What do I do best? That is, what are my strengths, or the things I most enjoy doing?

3. What other things will influence my decision? Perhaps:

   - the opinions of family and friends?
   - the availability of employment?
   - staying in the local area?
   - salary?

If your mentee remains unsure, encourage them to complete a career survey using a credible website—this is where the support of a mentor is invaluable—or introduce them to someone skilled in career guidance you might know for further discussions. Magdalena Brzezinska and Edward Cromarty offer a strategy to assist guiding students who might be in challenging situations, which can be adapted in mentoring situations, or in schools and tertiary institutions, especially with the help and support of program staff or other relevant professionals:

Improving the teachers' ability to provide positive environments in crisis situations will assist Social Emotional Learning enhancing the development of student attention, decision-making skills, relationships, well-being, performance, and holistic growth. One technique that may assist in accomplishing this is holding a private interview and together creating a flexible learning agreement that promotes the development of each student ... to establish adjustable goals that engage and motivate.[1]

Tips to share with your mentee about how to manage their learning as preparation for the world of work

- *If it is meant to be it is up to me.* Take the first steps to become proactive with your learning.
- Life becomes more complex as you get older and your "Life Roles" increase. This requires decision making and prioritizing about how to use your time.
- Focus and delayed gratification—something takes longer to achieve than one hopes or expects—are concepts to understand for success.
- Allocating amounts of time to assignments, starting the process early, and being realistic about how much you can achieve in that time reduces stress.
- Focus on what needs to be done now, and you won't need to worry about the future.
- 100 billion neurotransmitters x 50,000 connections, run on 10 watts of electricity is a lot of brain power. You have so much potential.
- When your anxiety or stress levels are high, the executive function of your brain (the prefrontal cortex which is only fully developed by your mid-twenties) is suppressed by the release of hormones, and makes it harder to think.
- Lack of sleep, a poor diet, or poor planning, might negatively impact your memory. Planning, listening, and recall, are all needed for exams and assignments.

---

1. Brzezinska and Cromarty, *Emergency Remote Teaching*, 43.

CAREER THOUGHTS

Achievable strategies to share with young people preparing for the world of work

- Work together with peers to increase access to resources, and improve your understanding of the task or assignment.
- Consolidate memory by revising work within twenty-four hours, particularly in subjects like chemistry, mathematics, and physics.
- Tell someone else what you think, and question the information.
- Link the information to what you already know in any area of your life.
- Creative subjects need time for the intuitive creative brain (right hemisphere) to develop imaginative concepts—start planning early.
- Work smarter, not for longer periods of time; integrate your study throughout the day by talking to friends, teachers, mentors, and parents, and jot down inspirational thoughts as they come to you.
- Manage your time effectively. Seek help from someone you trust if you need assistance in this area.
- A study lifeline: communicate with a "study buddy" only to have academic or assignment questions answered, not to waste valuable academic study time having a lengthy unrelated social chat.
- A powerful learning tool is working together—help others and help yourself. This creates a positive win-win situation. Employees are always looking for "team" members.
- Lastly, *balance*—laugh, move around, look at the stars, smile, sleep, and focus on what you need to do today and tomorrow, as a part of your future. Enjoy *now*. It is a time in your life that will never happen again.

Reflection

Every decision in the world is made by the person who has the power to make a decision. Make peace with that.

—PETER DRUCKER

2. Career-related questions to discuss with young people [1]

Potentially great discussions can occur with young people when they are asked about possible careers beyond their school days. There is an opportunity for a mentor to share their personal journey about their career choices when they were teenagers, a chance to explore careers online, perhaps even the opportunity to attend a career exhibition in the community. Here are some questions to prompt such discussions.

1. What are your priorities at the moment?
2. How have you been doing in your school work during the past three months? Compare your results. What are your strong and weak subjects? What subjects do you enjoy? Why? What subjects don't you enjoy? Why not? What can we do to improve things for you?
3. So, you think your school work isn't great and you want to leave school? Have you thought about the importance of gaining the best education you possibly can for your long-term career prospects? Let's explore your options before you choose your future pathway.
4. Are you using a paper diary? I am happy to show you my diary, and we can explore ways of managing your time more effectively so you end up with more free time.
5. How much homework or extra study do you have? How are you handling it? Are there any ways I can support you, or are there any resources you need?
6. How much sleep do you get at night? When do you concentrate best in class, at work, or during your training (as applicable)?

1. Cox, *CHOICES*, 157-159.

CAREER-RELATED QUESTIONS TO DISCUSS

7. Let's look at the way you spend your time each week. I'll share how I manage my time if you would like me to do so.

8. Your examinations start in three weeks. Let's draw up a realistic revision schedule together.

9. Are you a member of your local library? When did you last go there? Would you like me to go with you? Perhaps we could check out what is in the library on possible careers for you, or your interests? If you want to join, I can help.

10. What subjects do you think you will study after school? What careers can you follow with these subjects? Would you like some help with long-term planning?

11. What are your options for further study after school? Would you like to explore possibilities?

12. Imagine you have only two years left on earth. What would you want to achieve by the end of that time, so that people will appreciate the difference you have tried to make?

13. Do you have a part-time job? What is it like? How many hours each week are you working? What do you like, or not like about it? Are you saving any money? Should we discuss how to budget?

14. If you are applying for a part-time job, you need a resume. Would you like me to help you draw up a winning resume?

15. If you could do any job, what would you be doing five years from now?

16. One day, if you could have a world-wide reputation for something, in what area would you like it to be? Why?

17. If you were going to leave the world one piece of advice before you die, what would you say?

18. What would your second career choice be? Why?

19. Name one person you admire (living or dead) who had to overcome great obstacles to achieve their dreams? How has their story impacted your life?

20. Can you think of a time when you were part of a team that won something? What happened, and what made it so special? Are there any lessons from the experience you think could be useful when you enter the workplace?

SECTION FOUR: PREPARING YOUNG PEOPLE

21. What ability do you wish you had that you don't? Why? What can you do about this?

22. Which mentor—someone in a mentoring, or coaching, or teaching role—has had the greatest impact on your life to date? Why, or how?

23. What is your favorite hobby? What other hobbies have you had in the past?

24. What career do you think your grandparents would like you to choose? A professional sportsperson? A TV or movie star? A famous explorer? A famous artist or inventor? A famous politician, or some other profession? What would your parents say?

25. Who is the best teacher you have had to date? Why?

26. What do you do during physical education lessons at school? How important are these lessons to you? If your school does not offer physical education, why do you think they should do so?

27. Do you have a cellphone? How much time do you spend on it?

28. Do you play video games? How often? What is your favorite video game? Would you like to discuss ideas about the responsible use of technology?

29. There is a saying, "honesty is the best policy." Do you agree with this? Why or why not?

30. Do you have one special sport or other non-academic school achievement? Tell me about it. Have you won other academic or school awards?

31. What are your favorite books? Why this choice? What is one favorite book?

32. Which famous historical figure has inspired you? How? Why this person?

33. What is the one thing you do really well most of the time? (It can be anything.)

34. You are in a basketball, or volleyball, or netball team. Would you prefer to win by forty points or six points? Share your thoughts.

35. You have been elected President or Prime Minister of your country. You have the authority to do any three things you choose. What would you choose to do, and why?

CAREER-RELATED QUESTIONS TO DISCUSS

36. A TV company has called you. You are given the opportunity to participate in any TV program of your choice. Which program would you choose? Why? Which character would you like to play?

37. What do you like and dislike about your school, or work, or further training?

38. How important do you think your schooling or education is in preparing you for your future career? Why?

39. Have you ever failed at something at school in recent times? How did you deal with it? What can you learn about yourself from the experience?

40. How important do you think breakfast is for your health and wellbeing, studies, or work? What do you have for breakfast each day?

41. Are there any issues at work you need to deal with (where relevant)? Do you have any strategies to deal with these challenges?

42. If you were made a teacher for a day, which subject would you want to teach? Why?

43. Which clubs in or outside of school do you belong to?

44. What musical instruments do you play, or have you played in the past? Is there a musical instrument you would like to play?

45. Which languages can you speak or understand?

46. What scares you the most about the future?

47. How do you respond to the statement that "money can buy you happiness"?

48. How much do you know about budgeting? Would you like me to share some thoughts and budgeting experiences?

49. Do you fear failure? When or where have you failed in your life to date? How do you feel about this?

50. How effectively do you feel your school is teaching you the skills you will need to succeed in life? What skills do you think are important for your life journey?

51. If you were an employer, what qualities would you look for in an employee in addition to the skills required for a particular job?

Reflection

If you really want to give your children [mentees] a few worthwhile gifts in this life, leave them with a sense of curiosity, good manners and a considerate nature. You will have made a bequest of inestimable value.

—Clive Simpkins

3. Support a young person to build a winning resume

I recall an occasion when I was working with some fifteen-year-old students trying to put together their resumes. Some were thinking of applying for part-time or casual work, while others wanted to start developing a resume so that, when they wanted work, or to apply for an apprenticeship, for example, they would be ready to do so.

As we looked at contact details, I saw that one young man's email address was crude. Indeed, most people would have found it offensive. This young man thought that it was amusing. When I told him that an employer would not bother to continue reading his resume when an email address like this appeared, he was visibly surprised.

When my son was about nineteen, he wanted to change jobs and asked me to check his resume. This I did, and informed him that he was unlikely to be invited for an interview. Initially he was angry with me, but when I started asking him why he had not included something like his Forklift Driver's License, he began to see where he had fallen short. What I was trying to tell him was that he had totally undersold himself—he had more talent, and had achieved so much more than was evident on his resume. He rewrote the resume, was invited for an interview, and offered a job which saw his salary rise by about $16,000 per annum (a large increase in those days).

Strategies and tips to support a young person to develop a winning resume

Think about what you put into your resume. Many employers only want a one-page resume, which obviously restricts what you can include.

SECTION FOUR: PREPARING YOUNG PEOPLE

Sell yourself by including as much relevant information as you can. For example, don't just say you played baseball or basketball. Include the fact that you played for the same club team for six years, and mention any awards, or honors you achieved. This shows that you have qualities such as perseverance, loyalty, teamwork, and commitment, qualities that most employers look for.

A few more points to consider as you put together your resume:

- Each time you include a point on your resume, ask yourself this question: *Will this item help me get an interview?*
- Always deliver or post a hard copy of your resume—where this is possible—if you are not completing an application online. If you send your resume by email, send your resume as a .pdf attachment (unless otherwise requested). You might want to check with the potential employer that your email will be opened, as some businesses don't open attachments from people they do not know.
- As you put your resume together, ask yourself how useful your information might be to a prospective employer.
- Finally, expect to be rejected when you apply for jobs. In other words, don't expect every employer to invite you for an interview. You are only one of many applicants, and there is only one job available. Never take rejection personally, and don't quit applying. The person who perseveres and explores different options, different types of jobs, even jobs that they might not really want, but sees that a job could kickstart their career, are the people who will work smart, and make progress up the career ladder.

When my son was a young adult, he taught me a great life lesson about finding a job. "Dad, anyone can find work if they are prepared to roll up their sleeves and do a job they might not ever really want to do. Jobs are out there."

Have realistic expectations.

Most of us started at the bottom of that ladder and worked our way up. I began by parking cars in the street where I lived when international sports matches were taking place at the local stadium. The drivers gave me a tip because I had saved them time by pointing to a space to park their car. Then I buttered rolls, sold soft drinks, and cleaned up the litter left by about four thousand spectators at that same stadium. When I was a little older,

I worked for the City Council checking data—a tedious job, yet I earned sufficient to purchase my first car. Finally, I graduated from university and had the best career ever, a teacher!

A word of encouragement to mentors. I recall listening to a mentor share with another group of newly trained mentors his experience working in this area of preparing young people for the world of work with the teenager he was mentoring who lacked self-confidence, yet wanted to obtain some part-time work. The mentor helped the mentee create his resume, and then went into a shopping mall one afternoon to see if there were any jobs available. By the time they walked out of the shopping mall, the mentee had secured a part-time job, possibly also a life-changing experience for that young man.

Reflection

A mentor is not a social worker or a savior. A mentor is a guide . . . Therefore, you will have to find the fortitude to resist the urge to solve your mentee's problems or to "rescue" them from the circumstances of their lives. That is hard to do when you become emotionally invested in the life of a child. Yet, to fulfil your proper role as a mentor, you will have to summon the courage to remain an empathetic guide as your mentee deals with problems, makes choices, commits errors, and develops the inner resources necessary to rise above circumstances and turn challenges into opportunities.

—Thomas W. Dortch Jr.[1]

---

1. Dortch, *The Miracles of Mentoring*.

4. Support a young person to create a winning cover letter and portfolio

Many young people—and adults—fail to see the importance of the cover letter which accompanies a resume when one is applying for a job. These days a persuasive cover letter is almost more important than the resume. Why? Because before looking at the resume the employer must be persuaded to do so. This is hugely important especially when there are many people applying for the same job in a competitive market.

The post-pandemic economy throughout the world is battling, unemployment numbers are rising in many areas, and, naturally, there will be many more people looking for jobs. One must think smart, and be organized. A well written cover letter can often be the difference between being invited to an interview, or not receiving that telephone call.

Here are a few key points to share with a young person when they write a cover letter:

- Keep it short, to the point, and powerful.
- Change the contents to fit *each* job you apply for.
- Sell yourself and your suitability for the job—always with integrity.
- Show your enthusiasm.
- Be genuine, positive, and upbeat.
- Sometimes an employer asks you to respond to certain criteria in the advertisement—perhaps, the employer wants someone with specific computer skills, and experience in a particular area. Make sure you respond to the criteria.

- Make sure everything relevant to the job you are applying for, and which you mention in your cover letter, is supported with more information in your resume.

You have your cover letter, your resume, and then, perhaps, you have a separate page or pages referring specifically to the criteria listed for the job for which you are applying. Much of what you write here will be evident in the content of your resume—as mentioned above—and that's great.

Many people can't be bothered responding to the criteria and send off their resume in the hope that will be enough. An experienced employer will ignore the resume. After all, if you can't be bothered to respond properly to the advertisement, what is that saying about you as a potential employee?

It's little things like this that make such a significant impact when one is applying for jobs.

Support a young person put together an impressive portfolio

Jeff was mad about cars. At the age of fifteen he purchased a car for $500. It was not roadworthy and needed a lot of work. Over the next two years Jeff worked many hours to have the car ready for registration for use on the road. He totally overhauled the engine, spray painted the exterior, and refurbished the interior. This was indeed a labor of love, but then Jeff was passionate about cars, remember.

I met Jeff when he was putting together his resume, cover letter, and portfolio. We even did a mock interview, imagining I was the employer and he was applying for a mechanic's job in my business.

As I conducted the interview and started asking Jeff questions about his knowledge of cars, his eyes lit up and he shared how he had built this wreck into a registered car, now able to be driven on the road. His passion for cars was clear, his willingness to persevere in a job that he was passionate about obvious. Indeed, at the age of seventeen he probably knew far more about cars than most young people of his age—and many adults, too, for that matter—*and* he had something to show for his passion.

This is where the portfolio can be important. Jeff was able to place on the table photographs of the car when he bought it, the various stages of repair, and then the car ready and registered to go on the road. For someone looking for a mechanic, *there* was the evidence.

You might be thinking that this could always be a con job and there was no proof that Jeff had done this work. Wrong! Jeff had included the names of two referees who would vouch for the fact that he had spent two years restoring this car.

I don't think Jeff had too many difficulties finding an apprenticeship in the motor trade.

Start now by encouraging your mentee to gather all their certificates and awards, and place them in a plastic sleeve, or a file where they are safe. I have met many young people who told me that they had been awarded certificates for something they achieved, but could not find these when they looked for them. There is little point in placing this information in your resume if you are unable to prove that what you have written is the truth.

Some students wonder why it's important to include their latest school reports. An employer might want a quick look at a school report to see what teachers are saying about the applicant, as, outside of their family and immediate friends, their teachers probably know them better than most. Many employers place a lot of value on teachers' comments when hiring young people for work.

In addition, they might want to look at the number of days the applicant has missed school, as this will give them an indication as to how often they might be at work. Of course, if the applicant was genuinely ill, for example, they would explain that, and invite the employer to telephone the school to verify their statement. By suggesting this, the applicant will display their honesty, a quality that all employers are looking for in their employees.

Organize the portfolio so that the applicant can easily find the information during an interview and, remember, never leave an employer with an original, only a copy.

A portfolio *might* be the key difference between a job offer, or a job offer wasted.

Support and encourage your mentee to be organized, and start planning today. They will save so much time later.

Reflection

Everything can be taken from a man or woman but one thing: the last of human freedoms—to choose one's attitude in any given set of circumstances, to choose one's own way.

—Victor Frankl (Holocaust survivor)

5. Share effective job interview skills for the work place with young people

Anyone working with young people can play a significant role in encouraging and supporting them when they head off to a job interview. Here are some thoughts to guide that process.

No matter your age, it is normal to feel nervous when going for a job interview. However, if you are organized and have planned well for the interview, you will be better prepared and able to settle into the interview quickly.

I recall one time when I went for an interview, I spent about a day researching information about the school where I hoped to gain employment. I browsed the school's website, read recent newsletters, skimmed through annual reports, and read a variety of other articles.

Before I had even applied for the job, the principal had encouraged people interested in the job to contact him if they had questions. I took advantage of this offer and was able to ask a number of questions, which not only let him know that I was enthusiastic about applying for the job, but also that I had a great deal of education experience, and was not afraid to ask some tough questions.

When I arrived for the interview, I felt that I already knew the principal, and I certainly knew a lot about the school. I was able to ask some good questions, when given the opportunity to do so, while also referring to information on the school website when I was responding to the questions. This was important, as the job involved some research. I was showing the interview panel that I enjoyed research.

I had also discussed the job with my wife, and she had shared possible questions I could be asked, some of which I had not thought about. Indeed, I think one of these, which was later asked in the interview, was hugely important and might have helped me attain the job.

SECTION FOUR: PREPARING YOUNG PEOPLE

Winning interview strategies and tips to share with young people

Here are some interview strategies and tips to share with a young person when they start applying for a job.

- Sleep for at least nine hours the night before the interview.
- Eat a good breakfast.
- Be punctual—arrive at least ten minutes before your appointment.
- Dress appropriately, "as if you were already working in that field."[1]
- Take care of your personal hygiene and appearance.
- Don't smoke (vape), chew gum, or eat during the interview.
- Switch off your cellphone, and put away any other devices.
- Be polite, courteous, and friendly to *all* support staff—above all, *be yourself* at all times.
- When meeting the interviewer or interview panel:
  - Keep eye contact throughout the interview, and don't rush your answers.
  - Remember the importance of body language (both yours and that of the interviewer).
  - Don't fidget.
  - Be pleasant, friendly, warm, and polite.
  - Listen carefully to questions, and don't interrupt the interviewer. If you don't fully grasp what is being asked, request clarification.
  - Don't volunteer negative information about yourself. Psychologist and author Andrew Fuller offers a helpful strategy and tip:

    > Give the employer one or two notable ways to remember you. It could be an interest you share in common, or it could be that you outline how you will contribute as soon as you start the job. If you bring a specific skill, show how it could be used to help out.[2]

---

1. Fuller, *Tricky Teens*, 286.
2. Fuller, *Tricky Teens*, 287.

- Express your genuine interest in the job. Prepare at least three questions to ask at the interview—for example, when can I expect to hear whether my application is successful? What future opportunities might there be for me within this organization once I have been here for a while? Don't be afraid to ask questions for clarification.

- After the interview send an email thanking the interviewer for inviting you to the interview—another message that you are genuinely interested in the job.

More supportive strategies and tips to prepare for the interview

Some other quick tips for young women which have been recommended by many people who have worked in this field:

- No low-cut blouses or tops.
- No mini-skirts, or inappropriate clothing.
- Don't overdo the makeup, or jewelry.

Some extra tips for young men from many employers:

- Wear buttoned shirts, and make sure the shirt is fresh and ironed.
- Preferably dark trousers, not jeans.
- No sports shoes or sneakers.
- Wear socks.
- Don't overdo the deodorant, or after-shave.

Some extra tips for possible discussion with young people:

- Get rid of too many studs—they don't impress employers.
- Where possible, cover any tattoos—some customers find these offensive.
- Comb your hair away from your eyes; tie your hair back from your eyes neatly—employers want to see your eyes, as they are an expression of your personality.
- Some employers don't like long hair (boys), so check out the potential place of employment before you go for the interview. I heard the story of a young man, hugely talented and with a university degree,

who kept being invited for interviews and then missing out on the job. When, in desperation, he finally phoned an employer and asked why he had failed yet again, the employer simply responded, "have a haircut." He had a haircut and was offered the next job he applied for.

- Remember that all staff you meet should be regarded as part of the interview panel, not just the time you spend with an employer being interviewed.

No one owes you or me anything and this is something a lot of young people battle to understand. I have heard many teenagers say things like, "this is who I am. I am not going to change," or, "I have my rights." If they are continually turned down when they apply for jobs, perhaps they might have to look in the mirror again.

Finally, remember that an employer will make a judgment about you in the first thirty seconds they meet you. It is, therefore, vital that you prepare thoroughly for the interview, present yourself well, engage in eye-to-eye contact immediately, have a firm and confident handshake, and have an enthusiastic smile on your face when you meet your potential employer for the first time.

Reflection

Just listening can be a far greater gift than the listener realizes, whatever the age of the person being listened to. Listening to another person is a way of giving him or her worth, of valuing them. It is not second best to speaking. It is a gift in its own right and something we can all do. When I listen to someone carefully, I give space to allow them to express themselves. This can be a great gift in today's busy life when everyone is in a hurry.

—Anne Long[3]

---

3. Long, *Listening*.

6. Top motivators for employers of young people

I am grateful for the people who moved alongside me and guided me in a variety of ways when I entered the workforce during difficult and challenging economic and political times. There were so many unknowns—what was the future looking like? How do I budget? Who can I trust? Who do I approach for guidance? Am I really up for this job?

Can you remember the people who influenced you the most when you joined the work force? How has the workplace today differed from when you entered it for the first time? How would you motivate, support and encourage a young adult joining your team in their first career move?

Neuroscience research continually reminds us that the brains of youth are only fully developed when they are in their mid-twenties. This highlights how important it is for empathetic employers to guide and navigate new young employees entering the work place for the first time.

I spent some time researching employer and employee relationships, exploring what social researchers say, and reading general articles in which employers share their experiences working with young people. I have observed over the years how the advent of technology seems to change the mindset of young employees.

In some cases, I saw young people unafraid to be creative and innovative. In other situations, I observed young people unable to empathize with others, severely lacking teamwork skills, and often with questionable management of time skills. I saw others who took life so seriously, were unable to laugh at themselves, and whose perfectionist attitude led to heightened stress levels. I observed others who lacked a healthy and balanced lifestyle, which had a negative effect on their output. And, I noted others who had no idea how to cope with the challenges of the workplace, and either left the work place voluntarily, or were asked to move on.

SECTION FOUR: PREPARING YOUNG PEOPLE

Here are fourteen top motivators to support employers of today's youth—and which are valuable discussion topics between mentors and mentees—always remembering that every employee is unique, different, and brings their personal life story to the workplace.

1. Young people value flexibility in terms of hours of work.
2. Offer access to state-of-the art training opportunities which are preferably experiential rather than only online learning. Young people often require "soft skills" learning to build meaningful relationships with other employees, customers, or clients—presentation skills, management skills, management of time skills, communication skills, and team-building skills.
3. Encourage mentoring opportunities, whereby a wise guide moves alongside a young person, is non-judgmental and empathetic, and inspires them to chase their dreams, and reach their potential.
4. Mentoring is a great vehicle for values sharing and knowledge transfer. Young people listen and observe everything going on around them, even when one thinks this is not the case.
5. Young people respond positively to inspiring and motivational leadership from authentic and trustworthy leaders. Marshall Goldsmith points out: "In my experience, fully engaged employees are positive and proactive about their relationship to the job. They not only feel good about what they're doing; they don't mind showing off their enthusiasm to the world."[1]
6. Recognition and reward—genuinely affirm a young person when they complete a task well, most especially commenting on their *efforts*.
7. Most young people enjoy the challenge of understanding cutting-edge technology. Explore ways you can use their skills to coach other colleagues, as this will create a wonderful collaborative team.
8. Young people genuinely appreciate honest, regular, and constructive feedback, though the timing of this feedback is also important in their personal development journey.
9. Make sure that young people have a clear understanding of their role in the big picture. They want their lives to have meaning and purpose.

---

1. Goldsmith, *Triggers*, 106.

10. Share messages of hope, and coach young people how to envision the future. Discuss with them how "instant gratification" and "entitlement" attitudes will not assist their personal growth; that failure occurs, and the key is *how* they learn from failure.
11. Make sure you offer an inclusive, participative, non-threatening team environment where they feel able to contribute, and their ideas and opinions are valued.
12. Develop an environment which acknowledges a young person's preferred style of learning: social, collaborative, interactive, and fun.
13. Encourage young people to live a healthy and balanced lifestyle, and offer some strategies and examples of how to attain this.
14. Encourage young people to stay informed about the dangers of substance abuse and the negative impact it is likely to have on their work environment and employment possibilities.

Employers can play a significant role in transforming many young lives which have been battered by the negative impact of the pandemic, lockdowns, environmental disasters, violence and war, the knocks to their self-confidence, and shattered dreams. Employers can be amazing mentors.

Reflection

Retired school principal Keith Richardson was asked whether he could have predicted the success of one of his proteges who completed his schooling, and became a renowned international sportsman. Keith's response:

> I am often asked whether I would have predicted his success. I always give the same answer:
> - I have seen so many boys with talent go through this school.
> - However, success demands more than talent.
> - Success demands a work ethic and a mental strength to divert criticism and to fight back from disappointment.
> - Success also demands humility and luck [good fortune].[2]

---

2. Richardson, *Before the wax melts*, 194.

7. The most important twenty-first-century emotional, entrepreneurial, and employability skills

What were the most important skills you needed for the world of work when you were at school? Did anyone ever discuss these with you? How did you decide what career to follow? How has the world changed since you were at school? Did you appreciate there were different roads you could travel to attain your career goals? Did anyone explain this to you?

We can probably remember times at school when we asked ourselves why we were studying a certain subject? How was it relevant to our lives beyond school? I used to ask this question often, as much of what I was learning appeared irrelevant and boring at the time—indeed, as I think back now, some of that work still seems to have been irrelevant or, perhaps my teachers did not show me the relevance to my life of what they were trying to impart. Maybe I was not listening. I was a normal teenager, yet today's world is demanding more creativity and innovation as the Digital Age expands and evolves.

I have thought about all these questions a great deal, read relevant books and articles, and worked with hundreds of young people, during which time we discussed these questions as we explored hopes and dreams. Author Tony Wagner[1] writes:

> The Millennials are our future. They are the generation who can and must create a healthier, more secure and sustainable way of life. While some might not care to admit it, they also need us in order to succeed. They need our expertise, guidance, mentoring and support, but we have to offer help in new ways .... to actively encourage the Innovation Generation to create an economy and a way of life based on innovation—one that cultivates habits

---

1. Wagner, *Creative Innovators*.

THE MOST IMPORTANT TWENTY-FIRST-CENTURY SKILLS

and pleasures of creative adult "play", rather than mindless consumption.

With these thoughts in mind, here are ten of the most important twenty-first century skills that most employers look for, and all young entrepreneurs require, along with other financial skills, and the skills specific to the particular job or career pathway they are exploring. Repetition is deliberate.

1. *Communication:* good written and spoken communication skills; great listening skills; trust; patience; an understanding of body language, tone of voice, and eye contact; able to question, network, and resolve conflicts positively, which is vital when designing new projects, and working with others; able to negotiate.

2. *Teamwork:* a great team player; an encourager; loyal; collaborative across many networks; strives to be a positive person of influence at all times, building others up; shows integrity at all times; patience; commitment; empathy and perseverance.

3. *Problem solving (includes complex problem solving):* able to work through difficulties and make decisions; collaborative; adaptable and flexible; open-minded; able to look at all viewpoints objectively and respectfully; motivated to give something back by striving to address a human need; imaginative; perseverance; prepared to risk failure while daring greatly.

4. *Initiative and enterprise:* able to follow through on one's ideas; creative, innovative and imaginative with a spirit of inquiry when looking for solutions, or developing new ideas; looking for extra work when tasks are completed (intrinsic motivation); able to work independently and as a team member; solution-focused; a critical and strategic thinker.

5. *Planning and organizing:* organized, self-disciplined, and takes a pride in presenting oneself for a job; great management of time skills; goal oriented; team player.

6. *Self-management:* as above and with a strong work ethic; accountable for one's work plans and taking ownership of one's responsibilities; reliable; trustworthy; prepared to take calculated risks; emotional intelligence.

7. *Learning:* a strong desire to keep learning, with an appreciation that life is a lifelong learning experience; an interest in study and research

to increase one's knowledge and understanding; listening to people with more experience; respecting diverse viewpoints; cognitive flexibility; personalized learning methods; an independent thinker; able to reflect on lessons from history and other cultures; willing to explore multidisciplinary learning methods; learns how to access and analyze information, and become an enthusiastic self-learner.

8. *Technology*: stays up-to-date with changes and developments in technology and its evolving role in the world of work; responsible and respectful use of social media; self-awareness of the role of one's digital footprint in the local and global community.

9. *Sense of humor*: work must be enjoyable and fun; one must be able to laugh with others, as well as laugh at oneself.

10. *A positive person of influence*: collaborative leadership; able to energize teams and other individuals; positive role model with strong morals and values; lives a healthy and balanced lifestyle; exercises regularly; above average relational skills; caring and compassionate; empathetic; able to reflect; authentic; great listener; humble; pro-active; self-confident; gives back to others with a sense of service (servant leadership); courageous; true to oneself.

There will be many points that can be added to this list.

This list also highlights the importance of encouraging young people to find volunteer adults they trust to move alongside them for a while as the wise guides on the side, the non-judgmental, supportive cheerleaders displaying the spirit of mentoring.

These young people *can* learn the importance of meaningful relationships in their lives, a developmental process that takes time, and which is important especially until their brains are fully developed into their mid-twenties.

Reflection

Being a friend means mastering the art of timing. There is a time for silence. And a time to let go and allow people to hurl themselves into their own history. And a time to pick up the pieces when it's all over.

—Gloria Naylor

8. The power of the spirit of mentoring—concluding thoughts

The more I mentored adolescents, the more I saw how the majority of our young people value a significant non-parent adult who believes in them. Some youth research has stated that young people need at least three significant adults in their lives during adolescence.

There are a variety of reasons for this. One important reason is that a mentor can provide a safe space for their mentee to talk about more personal and sensitive issues, some of which might include the family dynamics.

Who were the significant adult role models in your life during your adolescent years? And beyond?

As you reflect on the impact of this person or these people on your life, consider which mentoring qualities or characteristics they portrayed in their relationship with you.

Sixteen-year-old Emma was talented, hard-working, ambitious, and with a heart to reach out to those in need. She had been through tough times when her parents divorced and had built a protective wall around herself, not allowing too many people to get close to her in case she was hurt again.

I was informally mentoring Emma and supporting some charity projects she was facilitating.

A significant change in our relationship occurred one day when we were chatting and I simply commented: "Emma, you have a beautiful smile, especially when you smile through your eyes as well."

"Thank you," Emma responded with that smile.

From that moment on our relationship moved to a deeper level. Emma was more comfortable to share more of her personal experiences, her concerns, fears, and self-doubts. Together we developed strategies aimed at encouraging Emma to fulfil her considerable potential.

Emma also learned to laugh more, especially at herself. I loved the occasion when she walked out of my office, turned to me and said, "I don't take myself too seriously," yet she was a high achiever, motivated, and ambitious.

Emma completed a highly successful school career, excelled at university, and has great career possibilities.

While I was writing this book, I received a message from a student I taught in the 1990s. Leo wanted to phone me for a chat. Leo had been a young anti-apartheid activist in South Africa, and his education had been severely disrupted before he came to the school where I was the school principal. A businesswoman had befriended Leo and his mother, taken Leo under her wing, and made sure he gained an education that would allow him to chase his dreams.

Leo and I spoke on the phone for about an hour. Most of the time I listened. We had communicated very briefly after his school days. Leo told me that he had been critically ill, and there was a time doctors feared he would not survive. Thankfully, he pulled through.

Leo had been insistent that we speak, as he wanted to thank me for giving him a chance to gain an education during a difficult and challenging time of his life. Most especially, I had spoken to his immense artistic gifts and talents which gave him a real purpose for staying in school, as he was a couple of years older than his peers.

He reluctantly decided to leave South Africa to pursue his dream of becoming an international artist with his own studio. He lives the dream today, and gives credence to Mark Wolynn's supportive, and challenging perspective:

> A life completely devoid of trauma … is highly unlikely. Traumas do not sleep, even with death, but, rather, continue to look for the fertile ground of resolution in children of the following generations. Fortunately, human beings are resilient and are capable of healing most types of traumas. This can happen at any time during our lives. We just need the right insights and tools.[1]

Leo's story is a reminder to all who journey alongside young people, to name the strengths they see in these students, and to encourage them to chase their dreams. By doing so, they are developing the resiliency of youth.

1. Wolynn, *It Didn't Start*, 52.

THE POWER OF THE SPIRIT OF MENTORING

I will always be grateful to Colin Elliot for the supportive role he played over five years when I was a school principal.

Colin was a retired businessman, involved in a variety of community activities, always seeking to make a positive difference.

Colin believed in me. He supported the vision my colleagues and I had developed to see our school move forward during challenging political, economic, and education times in South Africa.

However, Colin was also authentic. He often challenged me with tough questions, a reminder that sometimes one needs to persevere, change one's mindset, look at a situation through a different lens, or make sacrifices to achieve a goal or vision.

Then, through his networks, Colin would inevitably open a door to a potential donor or supporter that would see an aspect of the vision able to be realized.

Colin was a wonderful mentor. He was my humble, non-judgmental cheerleader for a key season in my life. He coached and taught me much about selfless leadership—a superb role model.

About twenty years ago, a group of former school principals and a couple of other people actively involved in youth mentoring in New Zealand met to discuss the possibility of setting up a national organization to network with all youth mentoring agencies. This evolved into the New Zealand Youth Mentoring Trust.

During a tea break one of those attending, Jim Peters, and I were chatting about the development of youth mentoring. Jim had recently had a book published: *Building Resilience in Schools—An Introductory Handbook*. He clearly saw my passion for wanting to see our young people reach their potential, and knew I was training volunteer adult mentors at the time. He saw some writing potential within me that I definitely could not see.

Jim encouraged me to send a book proposal to his publishers. With great trepidation I approached the publisher, Essential Resources. They offered me a contract to write the book, *The Mentoring Spirit of the Teacher: Inspiration, support and guidance for aspiring and practicing teacher-mentors*. This was followed by five other mentoring books in partnership with Essential Resources.

I am indebted to Jim for believing in me and the work I was doing at the time, and giving me the nudge to approach a publisher, aware that there was a high risk of rejection. A great example of a man with wisdom, insight, and experience seeing someone's potential and speaking to that potential—promoting the spirit of mentoring, and continuing all these years later to encourage me to write this book.

How we move into the future, and how we influence the future remains a personal choice. *Every* life matters. *Every* life has a story. Remember the message behind the Cherokee Legend?

> An old Cherokee was teaching his grandson about life. "A fight is going on inside me," he said to the boy. "It is a terrible fight, and it is between two wolves. One is evil. He is anger, envy, sorrow, regret, greed, arrogance, self-pity, resentment, inferiority, lies, false pride, superiority, and ego.
>
> The other is good. He is joy, peace, love, hope, serenity, humility, kindness, benevolence, empathy, generosity, truth, compassion, and faith.
>
> The same fight is going on inside you and inside every person, too."
>
> The grandson thought about his words for a minute, then asked his grandfather, "Which wolf will win?"
>
> The old Cherokee simply replied, "The one you feed."

Who will you feed?

Reflection

… we must have the courage to follow young people as they lead—to see ourselves as individuals with the power to provide young people with what they need to lead us into the future. Angela Davis, a well-respected member of the ongoing civil rights movements in this country [USA], once said that "young people should be able to see further because they are standing on our shoulders." This quote is a reminder that young people benefit from the foundations we lay; that they can do their work because we do ours. But it also reminds us that young people can do future work—that they can not only pick up where we have left off but move us further into the future than we might have imagined ourselves.

—Torie Weiston-Serdan[2]

2. Weiston-Serdan, *Becoming a Better Mentor*.

Appendix 1: Annette McGavigan (1 June 1957 – 6 September 1971)

During the early months of 2023 my wife and I visited Derry in Northern Ireland. I spent time walking around the Bogside, the area of thirty years of conflicts between British soldiers and the Irish Republican Army (IRA), which ended with the signing of the Good Friday Agreement in 1998. The mural of Annette McGavigan moved me deeply, a reminder of the many young lives lost during unnecessary conflict situations when global leaders should do *everything* in their power to bring about world peace. My hope and prayer are that mentors, as they promote the spirit of mentoring in discussions with their mentees, will promote thinking about ways to attain global peace, end global poverty, treasure the environment, and put an end to the suffering of many innocent people of all ages.

Here is my brief tribute to the life of this beautiful young woman, who was taken from the world far too early, collated from my research.

Fourteen-year-old Annette lived with her parents, four brothers and two sisters, in Drumcliffe Avenue in the Bogside, Derry, Northern Ireland. She was a student at St. Celia's Secondary School during the conflict between British soldiers and the Irish Republican Army (IRA).

On 6 September 1971 Annette and her fellow students were sent home early from school due to continual rioting in the area. After the rioting had begun to diminish at approximately 6.00 pm, Annette, still wearing her school uniform, and holding an ice-cream in her hand, was shot in the back of the head by a British soldier, while standing at the corner of Blucher Street and Westland Street. It was thought she was bending down to collect the rubber bullets that many youths collected as souvenirs.

APPENDIX 1

Father Edward Daly, who gave Annette the last rites, later recollected: "I saw a young girl lying on the ground with an ice-cream beside her. She had been hit in the head and was on the point of death. I gave her the last rites and then had to break the news to her mother, who collapsed. It was very difficult. It made a very powerful impression on me."

There have been many unsuccessful efforts by Annette's family to pursue inquests relating to the circumstances and culpability of her death. No one has ever been charged, or brought to trial in relation to Annette's death, nor has the Ministry of Defence released intelligence documents relating to her death.

Annette's family described her as a bright, generous-hearted, and happy girl who loved art and music, wrote poems, and expressed an interest in the nursing profession.

On 1 September 1999, a Bogside mural of Annette, *Death Of Innocence*, was unveiled on the gable wall of a home on the corner of Lecky Road and Westland Road, close to Free Derry Corner. The Bogside artists stated that it was intended to be supportive of the peace process. The Good Friday Agreement signed in Belfast on 10 April 1998, was a multi-party agreement signed by most of Northern Ireland's political parties, and an international agreement between the British and Irish governments. This significant agreement brought to an end thirty years of conflict in Northern Ireland known as the Troubles.

The mural depicts Annette in her school uniform with an encircled, partly colored butterfly to the above right of her head. To Annette's right is a broken rifle, red in color, pointing downwards and surrounded by the color white. Annette, deliberately standing in what the artists considered an innocent pose, is a representation of all the children who have been killed during the Troubles, both Protestant and Catholic. Her shirt is the lightest color in the mural and her arms are angled in, both serving to draw the viewer's eye to her first. She stands out in front of the debris, separated from her turbulent environment, an image of an innocent child standing peaceably, and not participating in any violent actions, and is used to illicit sympathy—a reminder of the many innocent people caught up in conflicts through no choice of their own.

The Bogside artists wished to convey the message of condemnation of all guns. The gun in the mural, which takes up the entire length, was painted broken, and is an important symbol of the renouncement of violence, and also reflects the futility of continued armed conflict. The gun is also boxed off from the girl, separated from the rest of the mural.

In addition to the crucifix in the upper right-hand corner, there are a number of crosses visible in the debris—which were not deliberately included—perhaps suggesting that life and peace can rise from the devastation.

A final word—an extract from a longer statement on their website—from 'The Bogside Artists' about the murals they have created in Derry:

> What confers a unique provenance on our work is the fact that we, both as artists and as citizens, are part of the story we feel obligated to tell. The story of the Bogside is our story and vice versa. Hence our sympathies are with all of the people who have suffered in Northern Ireland whatever their class, creed, politics or belief systems. We believe that only when both communities of Catholics and Protestants have confronted the wounds they have inflicted on each other, and on themselves, can there be the possibility of healing or forgiveness.
>
> To tell it like it is and was is vital to this catharsis. Our murals stand therefore as the not too silent witnesses to the colossal price paid in suffering and brutalisation by a hopelessly innocent people in their struggle for basic human rights. The institutionalisation of sectarian exclusivity is the very essence of the conflict. It is a crime against both Catholics and Protestants. Our fervent wish is that the peace process will give us time to put right what has been so drastically put wrong. To this end we devote our craft and our energy, our imagination, our story and our hope.[1]

1. The Bogside Artists' website.

Appendix 2: Mentoring Matters

The material for Youth Empowerment Seminars (YES!)—now called Mentoring Matters—my community project set up in the late 1980s, has been developed in line with the findings of extensive global research about teenagers which I have conducted for over forty-five years. This research suggests that deep down most adolescents would like the following experiences:

To be cared for (loved)

- Young people wish to feel safe and secure.
- The more they are cared for, the more secure they feel.
- They wish to be surrounded by people who unconditionally care for them.
- They value the positive influences of peers and adults to encourage them to reach their potential.
- They are encouraged to appreciate that they are more likely to fulfil their potential when there are clear rules or boundaries in place (some of which can be negotiated). When they step over these boundaries there will be reasonable consequences.

To be valued

- The more young people are valued the more positive self-worth they experience.

- They are encouraged to feel they have some control over things that happen to them.
- Empowering them is proof that they are valued, respected, liked, and are regarded as valuable resources. [Remember that most young people are powerful without any assistance from an adult.]
- They value fun time to interact with peers and adults, which also involves the development of social skills.

To know that life has meaning and purpose

- Young people want to know that they matter, and that their lives have significance.
- The more they understand that there is a reason for their existence, the more significant they feel.
- They value encouragement to explore opportunities within and outside of school to learn and develop new skills and interests.
- They are encouraged to acquire a commitment to learning: academic success and the long-term value of learning enhances their self-worth as they discover their gifts and talents.
- They learn to appreciate and understand how to make the tough decisions and choices, and how to cope with new situations.
- They value guidance to develop a positive view of the future.

Appendix 3: Advancing the spirit of mentoring: the mixed-age tutor group[2]

Schools think they are dealing with prefabricated social issues that creep in from the turmoil of family life, gangs, social technology, and more, and so they respond accordingly. But a response is not the same thing as an intervention; bullying can be greatly reduced by designing it out rather than in. The following general considerations guide such a process:

1. Any intervention needs to occur before the students even get to the classroom and that is why mixed-age tutor groups are vital and where they come into their own.
2. This makes the first hour of school induction a critical time. How this is organized is of the highest importance if pro-school behaviors are to overcome any negative ones.
3. Tutor groups have to be mixed by age and ability. In dog whispering terms, the aim is to create a balanced and self-organizing and self-supporting pack!
4. In a *mixed-age* setting, two tutors meet a maximum of four students of the same age in their tutor group, not twenty-six students [or more] of the same age. This means they form a learning and support relationship first. The new students feel known and attached.
5. They then engage with four older students from the same group who do all the induction work, showing them the ropes. This enables a second set of learning relationships to form. The group changes the group. No games are played at this time! Every child is a leader and

---

2. Barnard, *Socially Collaborative Schools*, 65–67.

mentor. Empathetic relationships form. The child doesn't have to choose friends because they are there already.

6. Every adult employed by the school is a tutor regardless of his or her status, including the head or CEO. This aligns everyone with school purpose and builds a belonging system.
7. Every room in the school is used, allowing tutor group sizes to reduce to around eighteen students [or a maximum of between twenty and twenty-two students].
8. The younger students are now ready, after a very short induction, to go to the classroom.
9. Later, they will meet the rest of the tutor group, all of whom are experienced and understand the induction process and feel they belong in their mixed-age tutor group and are safe.
10. Tutors meet tutees for twenty minutes each day before morning break: they never teach Personal, Social, Health and Economic education (PSHE) but practice it every day with tutees by building secure and supportive relationships.

Readers can now see why and how the tutor becomes the information hub of the school, the synaptic link able to pull down from the system what is needed to maximize and support learning. This puts the tutor in an ideal position for summative assessment; the whole management structure of the school has to be reformulated around this central concept of information, flow, intervention, and ongoing support.

In a mixed-age environment, new students find themselves meeting people already empathetic toward them, by design. The child does not have to vie for friendships but joins a network (family) of fellow travelers all on different stages of their learning journey eager to help and empathize. This is not social engineering but simply a means of putting people in touch with who they were best meant to be, induction into a wider, safer, more supportive family-style network. In effect the school fulfils the intrinsic need of child development. … The power of the group changes the group.

Acknowledgments

This book is the culmination of almost fifty years as an educator, sport coach, mentor, and youth mentor program developer. During this time, I have gathered quotes, notes from conferences, "gold nuggets" of wisdom, and helpful strategies and tips from a variety of books, magazines, blogs, DVDs, websites, and general conversations with people.

The content of this book, therefore, is a tribute to the many people from a variety of backgrounds and professions who have shared their life experiences and wisdom either with me personally, or with the global community. Many of these people have generously shared their resources with me.

An extensive list of resources is available on my website, providing readers with more references for the content of this book. If I have inadvertently failed to acknowledge a source—which is quite possible, as I have gathered so many quotes and resources over the years—I would be most grateful if the reader would inform me so that I can rectify the omission. I have clearly indicated when the author of a source is unknown, and there are a few longer quotes where I have been unable to find the original source.

Special thanks to all those who offered to endorse this book, and whose encouragement and support inspired me to complete the task of writing the book. Michael Garringer not only wrote the Foreword, but also offered me some invaluable advice on the contents, and I am grateful to Peter Barnard for allowing me to quote his work extensively in Appendix 3.

I am grateful to Martin Melaugh and 'The Bogside Artists' in Derry, Northern Ireland—Tom Kelly, Kevin Masson, and William Kelly—for giving permission to use the moving image of Annette McGavigan in this book. Martin kindly supplied the image.

ACKNOWLEDGMENTS

A sincere thanks to my close friend, Peter Van Ryneveld, who has been my cheerleader, encourager, fellow idealistic dreamer, and confidant for over fifty years. Pete was a businessman, entrepreneur, philanthropist, and conservationist, who lived life to the full, loved being in the bush with the animals and birds, and travelling with the family, always keen to explore new frontiers. Pete was always the first to encourage me to write the books, and keep chasing my dreams. He was unable to comment on the final draft of this book, as he suddenly and sadly died after being diagnosed with an aggressive cancerous brain tumor. However, he found the time to pen these words of encouragement during his final weeks:

> There is no time like the present to benefit from a high-quality mentoring guide for both young people and those in the mentoring arena, which we almost all are as parents, educators, counsellors, or even just good friends. Robin's latest publication introduces more jewels from his vast experience as a teacher, a mentor, and a coach. It contains essential guidelines for a principle-based approach to mentoring that has yielded tangible success; and it offers numerous on-point techniques to help young people find more meaning and fulfilment in a post-COVID world. It is an invaluable sequel to his excellent *Mentoring Minutes*.

Matthew Wimer and the amazingly supportive team at Resource Publications, an imprint of Wipf and Stock, have backed the publication of this book at all times, and I am grateful for all their guidance and support. In particular, special thanks to Heather Carraher for all the assistance she generously offered while preparing the book for publication. Her willingness to accommodate my numerous requests significantly and positively impacted the end product.

Finally, my wife Jane has been my greatest supporter and cheerleader through all my writing. She has an exceptional ability to edit my writing, and make meaningful and constructive suggestions which always add value to the end product. Much love and thanks!

Bibliography

Barna, George. *Real Teens: A Contemporary Snapshot of Youth Culture.* Raleigh, NC: Regel, 2001.
Barnard, Peter. *Socially Collaborative Schools: The Heretics Guide to Mixed-Age Tutor Groups. System Design and the Goal of Goodness.* Maryland: Rowman & Littlefield, 2018.
Be a Mentor, Inc. https://beamentor.org.8010.
Biehl, Bobb. *Mentoring: Confidence in Finding a Mentor and Becoming One.* Brentwood, TN: Broadman and Holman, 1996.
The Bogside Artists' website: https://cain.ulster.ac.uk/bogsideartists/menu.htm.
Browning, Paul. *Principled: 10 Leadership Practices for Building Trust.* St. Lucia: University of Queensland Press, 2020.
Brzezinska, Magdalena, and Cromarty, Edward. *Emergency Remote Teaching in the University Context: Responding to Social and Emotional Needs During a Sudden Transition Online.* In *Social Computing and Social Media: Applications in Education and Commerce,* edited by G. Meiselwitz. HCII 2022. Lecture Notes in Computer Science, vol 13316. Springer, Cham. https://doi.org/10.1007/978-3-031-05064-0_3.
Buckingham, Jennifer. *Boy Troubles: Understanding Rising Suicide, Rising Crime and Educational Failure.* Sydney, NSW: Center for Independent Studies, 2000.
Coyle, Graham. *To Infinity and Turn Left: Exploring God's Purpose for Christian Teachers.* London: Independent, 2020.
Cox, Robin. *CHOICES: Encouraging Youth to Achieve Greatness.* Eugene, OR: Resource, 2021.
———. *Letter 2 a Teen: Becoming the Best I Can Be.* Invercargill: Essential Resources, (updated) 2017.
———. *Mentoring Minutes. Weekly Messages to Encourage Anyone Guiding Youth.* Eugene, OR: Resource, 2020.
———. *The Mentoring Spirit of the Teacher: Inspiration, Support and Guidance for Aspiring and Practicing Teacher-mentors.* Invercargill: Essential Resources, (updated) 2016.
———. *The Spirit of Mentoring: A Manual for Adult Volunteers.* Invercargill: Essential Resources, (updated) 2017.
Delpit, Lisa. *The Politics of Teaching Literate Discourse—in City Kids, City Teachers: Reports from the Front Line.* Edited by W. Ayers and P. Ford. New York: New Press, 1996.
Dortch Jr., Thomas W. *The Miracles of Mentoring.* New York: Broadway, 2000.
Duff, Jill. *Lighting the Beacons: Kindling the Flame of Faith in Our Hearts.* London: SPCK, 2023.

Bibliography

Ehmke, Rachel. With Catherine Steiner-Adair and Donna Wick. *How Using Social-Media Affects Teenagers.* https://www.childmind.org. Not dated.

Feinstein, Sheryl G. *Secrets of the Teenage Brain: Research-based Strategies for Reaching and Teaching Today's Adolescents (Second Edition).* Thousand Oaks, CA: Corwin, 2009.

Freedman, Marc. *The Kindness of Strangers: Adult Mentors, Urban Youth, and the New Voluntarism.* Cambridge: Cambridge University Press, 1993.

Fuller, Andrew. *Tricky Teens: How to Create a Great Relationship with Your Teen ... Without Going Crazy!* Warriewood, NSW: Finch, 2014.

Gallo, Carmine. *The Storyteller's Secret: How TED Speakers and Inspirational Leaders Turn Their Passion into Performance.* London: Macmillan, 2016.

Global Child Forum. *Protect A Generation: (Save the Children): The Impact of COVID-19 on Children's Lives.* Save the Children International. https://www.globalchildforum.org.

Goldsmith, Marshall, and Reiter, Mark. *Triggers: Creating Behavior That Lasts. Becoming the Person You Want to Be.* New York: Crown Business, 2015.

Greenfield, Susan. *Mind Change: How Digital Technologies Are Leaving Their Mark on Our Brains.* New York: Random, 2015.

Herrera, Carla, and Garringer, Michael, eds. *Becoming a Better Mentor: Strategies to Be There for Young People.* Boston, MA, January 2022. https://www.mentoring.org/resource/becoming-a-better-mentor.

Hutchcraft, Ron. *The Battle for a Generation.* Chicago, IL: Moody, 1996.

Institute for Mental Health Initiatives. *Competent Kids: A Guide for Fostering Resilience.* George Washington University, not dated.

James, Jennifer. https://www.livinglifefully.com/people/jenniferjames.htm. Not dated.

Jensen, Francis E., and Nutt, Amy. *The Teenage Brain: A Neuroscientist's Survival to Raising Adolescents and Young Adults.* New York: Harper, 2016.

Jucovy, Linda. *Same Race and Cross-race Matching.* Philadelphia, PA: Public/Private Ventures, 2002.

Lemery, Neal C. *Mentoring Boys to Men—Climbing Their Own Mountains.* California: Createspace, 2015.

Long, Anne. *Listening.* London: Darton, Longman & Todd, 1990.

Mayo Clinic staff. *Tween and Teen Health.* https://www.mayoclinic.org. Not dated.

McCook, Ross. *Heart for Youth Trust.* https://heartforyouth.org.nz/whatwedo.htm

———. Correspondence with Cox, Robin, August 2023.

MENTOR. https://www.mentoring.org.

Office of the Surgeon General. *Our Epidemic of Loneliness and Isolation: The U.S. Surgeon General's Advisory on the Healing Effects of Social Connection and Community.* 2023.

Paterson, Gordon. *There Is Genius in Passion. Reflections on Developing Competence and Self-belief Through Human Movement.* Tauranga: Ad Rem, 2014.

Phillips-Jones, Linda. *The Mentor's Guide. How to Be the Kind of Mentor You Once Had—Or Wish You'd Had.* Revised Edition. Grass Valley, CA: Coalition of Counselling Centers (CCC)/The Mentoring Group, 2003.

Phillips-Jones, Linda, Walth Jean Ann, and Walth Carlo. *100 Ideas to Use When Mentoring Youth: Activities and Conversations to Help Your Mentees Excel.* Grass Valley, CA: Coalition of Counselling Centers (CCC)/The Mentoring Group, 2001.

Rhodes, Jean E. *Stand by Me: The Risks and Rewards of Mentoring Today's Youth.* Trilateral LLC: Harvard College, 2002.

Bibliography

Richardson, Keith. *Before the Wax Melts: Musings of a South African Headmaster.* Cape Town, Independent, 2018.

Search Institute. *What We're Learning About Developmental Relationships.* https://www.search-institute.org.

Siegel, Daniel J. *Brainstorm: An Inside-Out Guide to the Emerging Adolescent Mind, Ages 12–24.* London: Scribe, 2014.

Sinetar, Marsha. *The Mentor's Spirit.* New York: St. Martin's, 1998.

Stoddard, David A. *The Heart of Mentoring: Ten Proven Principles for Developing People to Their Fullest Potential.* Colorado: Navpress, 2003.

Street, Helen. *Contextual Wellbeing: Creating Positive Schools from the Inside Out.* Subiaco, WA: Wise Solutions, 2018.

Street, Helen, and Porter, Neil, eds. *Better Than OK: Helping Young People to Flourish at School and Beyond.* Fremantle, WA: Fremantle, 2014

Turner, Tina. *Happiness Becomes You: A Guide to Changing Your Life for Good.* New York: HarperCollins, 2020.

UK Youth. *The Impact of COVID-19 on Young People & the Youth Sector.* https://www.ukyouth.org. January 2021.

US Education Department. *Yes, You Can: A Guide for Establishing Mentor Programs to Prepare Youth for College,* 1998.

Vos, Jeannette. *Self-Learning: The Future of Education—An Introduction to the Next Learning Revolution.* Unpublished manuscript. 2023.

———*The Learning Revolution 2.0: Self-Learning Revolutionary Methods to Change the Way the World Learns, Thinks, and Leads.* Unpublished manuscript. 2023.

Wagner, Tony. *Creative Innovators: The Making of Young People Who Will Change the World.* New York: Scribner, 2012.

Walsh, David. *Why Do They Act That Way? A Survival Guide to the Adolescent Brain for You and Your Teen.* New York: Free Press, 2005.

Weinberger, Susan. *Dr. Mentor's 16 Steps to Effective Mentoring.* https://mentorconsultinggroup.com/publications Not dated.

———. *Lessons Learned: Two Decades of School-based Mentoring.* https://mentorconsultinggroup.com/publications. 2003. (updated 2023).

Wolynn, Mark. *It Didn't Start With You: How Inherited Family Trauma Shapes Who We Are and How to End the Cycle.* New York: Penguin, 2017.

Youth.gov. https://www.youth.gov.

www.ingramcontent.com/pod-product-compliance
Lightning Source LLC
Chambersburg PA
CBHW070742160426
43192CB00009B/1547